# Photoshop

1

# Photoshop

Mac Edition

Cathy Abes

VENTANA
PRESS

**Photoshop f/x: Mac Edition**
Copyright © 1994 by Cathy Abes

Library of Congress Cataloging-in-Publication Data

Abes, Cathy
    Photoshop f/x / Cathy Abes. — 1st ed.
            p.        cm.
    Includes index.
    ISBN 1-56604-179-1
    1. Computer graphics.  2. Adobe Photoshop.  I. Title.
    T385.A237  1994
    760—dc20                                                    94-22954
                                                                CIP

Book design: Marcia Webb
Cover design: Doug Grimmett, Dawne Sherman
Index service: Dianne Bertsch, Answers Plus
Technical review: Jim Allman; Julieanne Kost
Editorial staff: Angela Anderson, Walter R. Bruce, III, Tracye Giles, Pam Richardson, Jessica Ryan
Production staff: Patrick Berry, Cheri Collins, Ron Jackson, Dan Koeller, Dawne Sherman, Marcia Webb, Mike Webster
Proofreader: Alexa Dilworth
Section Page Images: Jeff Brice, p. 1; Jeff Brice, p. 111; Ruth Kedar, p. 221; Bonny Lhotka, p. 315

First Edition 9 8 7 6 5 4 3 2
Printed in the United States of America

Ventana Press, Inc.
P.O. Box 2468
Chapel Hill, NC 27515
919/942-0220
FAX 919/942-1140

**Limits of Liability and Disclaimer of Warranty**

# About the Author

Cathy Abes is an associate editor for *Macworld* magazine who covers Macintosh graphics. An eight-year veteran of *Macworld*'s editorial staff, she took over the monthly Art Beat column in 1990 and has been writing its successor, Expert Graphics, since it debuted in 1993. In that time, she has interviewed and written about many of the most talented and recognized Macintosh artists working today.

Abes organized and directed the 1991 and 1992 Macworld World-Class Awards and has developed and moderated graphics-related panels for Macworld Expo in San Francisco and Boston.

# Trademarks

# Acknowledgments

This book could not have been produced without the cooperation of the many talented artists who generously provided me with so many wonderful images. They spent many hours talking to me about what they did, how and why; compiling interim images in the proper formats—in some cases, recreating them; and producing detailed notes about their creative techniques. I'm indebted to them for all their help and for the invaluable insights they provided. I'm also grateful to Jim Allman of Images Associates, Matt Brown and Julieanne Kost of Adobe Systems, and Greg Vander Houwen for their technical help in preparing this book. I'd also like to thank Ventana Press for giving me this opportunity, and my project editor, Jessica Ryan, for being so patient and accommodating during this long, arduous process. Finally, my heartfelt thanks go to my family, Ken and Daron, for putting up with my long work hours; I couldn't have done this without them.

# Dedication

For Daron and Ken; my mother and father, Eleanor and Philip Abes; and my aunt and uncle, Marilyn and Reed Parker.

# Table of Contents

# Foreword

## by Kai

Photoshop makes photos hop—through impossible hoops. You know that. Except, you may not have an *exact* idea of just *how* to hop or which hoops it can *really* do.

These days it's widely known that most images we see around us have gone through various stages of digital assembly, clean-up, post-processing, special effects or all of the above. One cannot help feeling that it hardly even requires a camera anymore—a blank picture and Photoshop seem enough to concoct almost anything imaginable!

But, it's not quite as straightforward as all that. There are countless Photoshoppers out there who have invested half their lives in finding out the little secrets, the big idea, the hidden traps and the cool new tricks.

There's little point in reinventing the wheel, or reinvesting hours in the color-wheel even. You wouldn't explore a big city without a map, and that's why it's a *wheel* good idea that you have this book. It is a map of sorts. And Photoshop is a REAL big city.

Cathy Abes is of course in the real thick of this. As the author of *Macworld*'s Expert Graphics column, she has seen a thing or two come across her desk. Or two thousand. And really the key to this book is her contact with dozens of artists around the country, doing what hopefully you endeavor to do as well: push the pixels around till the image talks to you and says "Hold it! Don't touch me! I'm done...!"

Of course all good artists never really finish their works, they merely abandon them. This has always been my biggest problem, where to stop? Is THAT really the BEST texture on that headline or mayyyybeeeee....

Anyway, this book is a collection of images that artists from all over the country have poured their souls into. Some came easy. Some were so hard to do that the artist got a tan from the glowing phosphor. But they'd never admit that to you now of course. Half the art is to make it look effortless, as if the gradient glows are just pouring out of your tablet.

I bet if you could secretly turn over the mice of these folks, you'd see some serious scratches, wear and tear, all the hard disk crashes and file errors and lacking RAM and lost files....If you are a beginner, don't let that scare you, you'd never get started.

Much like with childbirth, if we knew everything beforehand, we'd be extinct by now! For you, maybe seeing the images and techniques revealed gives you a glimpse and hopefully encourages you to pick up the arrow and click on those buttons.

If you're in the middle of the Gaussian bell curve, the group of "I know Photoshop, sure" users, then you know that story about birthing pains all too well. But there is much to be learned still, trust me. Just look at each of the images and ask yourself "Could I recreate this? How would I do it...?" and you find that lo and behold there may be several ways to do the same thing, or just one way to do what you may have deemed impossible.

And if you are one of the top achievers, the killer "do-any-thing-anytime-hand-me-that-award" professional...well then you very likely have this book already anyway. Drinking information from a firehose may have been the tactic that got you the coveted spot near the elite in the first place. No one should ever be too proud to want to expand the horizons and absorb other peoples' work and the lessons they learned. If even you find just one little tip in the many pages here, it's already paid for itself.

So is there room for one more Photoshop book? You bet!

Three years ago, when there was exactly one, I was convinced that much of the deeper information would be appreciated by new users and old pros alike and I began writing up my own secrets as tips. In the spirit of altruism I uploaded them on America Online, slowly, a chapter at a time. After literally hundreds of thousands of downloads on networks globally, I have a pretty good feeling that there is still a very hungry group of people out there. So here is another tender morsel!

A word of advice though: There simply is no shortcut to experience. You will still have to log the hours and remember those option keys and deal with acronymia from DPI to CMYK and know that a Path in Photoshop may not lead to Rome or to salvation.

Enjoy reading Abes's book; it's not a passive bedside read though. Try to follow and redo and emulate and extrapolate. Send her a note about what you liked and how you have that simple 140-step procedure for Gold Embossing. Go into that cave where no one's been yet and discover the dead sea scroll bars. I'm sure that in another three years you still can find perfectly new ways to amuse your friends, annoy your spouses and delight yourself. Not to mention create images that no human has seen before. And that's no mean feat.

So many pixels, so little time.

# Introduction

Why another Photoshop book? you may ask. Aren't there enough already out there? True, there are plenty of books that catalog and explain how to use Photoshop's numerous features, that tell you which commands accomplish what amazing feats and what effects you can get from native filters and third-party plug-ins by applying each one in turn to the same image. If you're looking for an extension of—or a replacement for—the Photoshop user manual, one of those books should fill the bill.

But this book is different. What you'll find here, first and foremost, is a showcase of many unusual and beautiful images, done in a wide range of styles, by a wide range of experienced and talented artists, illustrators, photographers and photo-illustrators. It is also a generator of ideas; ideas drawn from the artists themselves as they show and describe the techniques they've discovered in the process of creating their images.

Photoshop users are a varied bunch, as evidenced by the group of artists represented here. Many use the program primarily for compositing scanned photographs and applying various effects to these digital collages; others use it to create images from scratch; still others combine scanned and original imagery. Some use Photoshop alone, while many use it in conjunction with other programs, such as Adobe Illustrator, Fractal Design Painter, Specular Collage or third-party plug-ins like Kai's Power Tools and Paint Alchemy. Photoshop is a program of such depth and breadth that it offers as much appeal to the photographer as the commercial illustrator and the fine artist. Anyone interested in graphic arts can find a reason to use it.

And now, with the long-awaited new version finally available, artists can accomplish even more with such features as layers, layer masks, color correction controls and interactive previews. Every image in this book was either originally created in Photoshop 3.0, recreated using 3.0 or updated to show how 3.0 features could have been used.

## Who Needs This Book?

Anyone working with Photoshop can benefit from this excursion into the creative processes of the more than thirty professional artists whose images are showcased here. Most have had their work appear in nationally known magazines and other publications; many have had their fine art images shown in galleries;

quite a number have had images displayed in other books as well. You'll find over one hundred of their images featured in these pages.

As any user can attest, there's rarely only one way to accomplish something in Photoshop. New techniques, new effects, new combinations of features are constantly being discovered, but no one person can discover them all. With its detailed step-by-step descriptions, this book will allow you to benefit from the expertise and adventurousness of skilled graphics professionals.

Whether you're a commercial illustrator or photographer or a fine artist, you'll find images and techniques that can push you in new directions, encouraging you to try new filters and effects—or old ones in new ways or combinations.

## What's Inside?

This book is divided into three main sections: the preliminary chapters and two galleries.

Chapter 1, "Photoshop 3.0: The New Features," focuses on Photoshop 3.0—its powerful new features and some pitfalls to watch out for. It includes case studies of images created in 3.0 using many of the new features, such as Layers, Color Range and Lighting Effects.

Chapter 2, "Special Effects with Third-Party Filters," is devoted to third-party plug-ins—filters developed by other companies to run within Photoshop. Not all such products are covered; descriptions of the most popular and widely known filters plus a couple of new entries are complemented by a number of case-study images showing the wide range of effects that can be produced with a little ingenuity and experimentation.

Chapter 3, "Using Other Programs With Photoshop," describes some of the other applications that are frequently used in conjunction with Photoshop, most notably, Illustrator, Painter, Collage and 3D programs. Again, images were selected as case studies to show the benefits of these combinations.

The Step-by-Step Gallery consists of images accompanied by extensive step-by-step tutorials, showing the illustration in progress and describing specific techniques developed by the artist.

The Gallery section is filled with images followed by an annotated description of the processes used to create them.

## How to Use This Book

Use this book to generate ideas for new ways of creating images and special effects. After you've gone through the preliminary chapters, go back to the sections that cover areas of particular interest to you. If you find an image that especially appeals to you, experiment with the techniques, filters and programs the artist used. Try out the filters and programs on the accompanying CD-ROM by experimenting with the sample images that are also included.

And remember, the point of following these step-by-step progressions is to expand your knowledge, experience and skill, not to reproduce exactly an image or effect. Also be aware that many filters produce different effects on images of different sizes and resolutions, so you may not instantly achieve the exact look you're after. Above all, these tutorials are meant to be used as stepping stones to develop your own techniques and forge your own style. So enjoy the process and begin creating your own wonderful images.

XVIII

# Section 1

## Case Studies

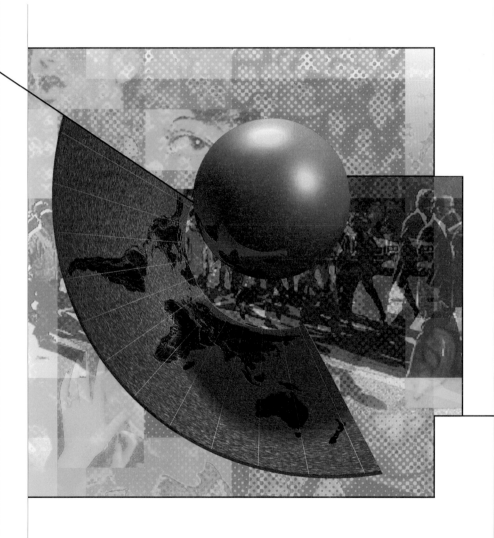

# CHAPTER 1

# Photoshop 3.0:
# The New Features

The long-awaited upgrade is finally here and it certainly seems to have been worth waiting for. Of course the biggest and most anticipated new feature is the ability to work in layers, which provides unlimited flexibility in image-editing and compositing, and the luxury of not having to linearly structure your images. But there are many more useful additions and changes in 3.0—plus some pitfalls to watch out for—described below.

## Layers

In 2.5 channels/masks or floating selections were the only way to work on an image without affecting the main underlying document. Now with Layers, Photoshop 3.0 makes it possible to work on separate image elements in full color, with each layer allowed a layer mask—an alpha channel applied only to that layer. Once you've applied a mask to a layer, you can create a new mask if necessary. The clear advantage to using layers is the flexibility in keeping design elements separate.

When you double-click on a layer, the Layer Options dialog box appears with a variety of blending modes to choose from, including most of the old ones and a few new ones (such as Hard Light and Soft Light, Overlay and Difference). Photoshop 3.0 allows layers to be controlled much like floating selections were with Composite Controls in 2.5 with floating and underlying tonal transparency (controlled by the Layer Sliders), modes and opacity. The difference, of course, is that compositing in 2.5 was a permanent process, while in 3.0 compositing between layers is infinitely undoable—until you "flatten" those layers. You can preview many layer interactions with varied modes and opacity settings as though the entire image were already composited. Just as with channels, you can show or hide any number of layers, reorder them, link them or clip them.

Painting in layers affects only the active layer; you cannot paint in multiple layers simultaneously. Layers can be made transparent with the Clear command (Edit>Fill>Mode:Clear). Rather than erasing an entire layer, it's preferable to erase portions of an image on a layer—making them transparent or semitransparent. You can, for example, make a window partially transparent or feather one image into another one. You can also protect the transparent areas by clicking the Preserve Transparency box on the Layers palette. You can create clipping groups to clip the background or base layer to the layer or layers above it. Similar to applying a layer as a mask, this is especially useful for mapping a texture onto an object in a layer.

Merge Layers leaves hidden layers unaffected, while Flatten Image discards hidden layers. Merge layers combines two or more layers, while flatten layers combines all the layers into one layer. Layer masks can be hidden by holding down the Command key and clicking on the mask. To view only the layer mask, option-click it. Assuming you have enough scratch disk space (which the layers depend on)—three to five times the file size is a good rule of thumb—you can maintain an image's elements in separate layers until you're sure no more changes are needed. In the lower left-hand corner of the file is a number that can reflect the scratch disk size needed as well as the image size with and without layers.

In 2.5 compositing an image was a very linear process, building from the ground up. Elements needed to be placed at just the right step in the image build; mistakes could be very costly and revisions usually meant hours of additional, painstaking work. The only way to go back a few steps other than Take Snapshot was to save a copy of the image or image area you wanted under a new name and to clone or fill back in from that version. Of course, the old method of floating images was much more economical.

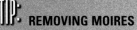

**TIP: REMOVING MOIRES**
David Peters often uses old photo scraps with large dot patterns. To eliminate the dot pattern and the resulting moire patterns, he photographs them again and scans in the photos.

**TIP: SAVING SPACE WITH LAYERS**
As people have no doubt begun to discover, layers can make a merely large file humongous. Both David Peters and Don Day have found that if you're compositing lots of elements, each on its own layer, you can easily wind up with a file that's 100mb or even larger that quickly gobbles up all your disk space. One way to minimize the storage drain is to build each element in a separate file with its own layers; then just add the finished element to the main image. Working with fewer and smaller layers at any given time keeps your files from getting unwieldy and your storage space under control.

Photoshop 3.0 users who use multiple layers can expect to invest in large hard disks to handle the additional storage layers will inevitably demand. The more layers, the more pixels and so the more hard disk space needed. Each layer in 3.0 takes up varying amounts of disk space, depending on the amount of information in the layer, the amount of transparency information and the number of tiles (sections of a layer) that contain information. For example, a layer whose tiles all contain information will be much larger than a layer with mostly empty tiles. As you might imagine, a 50mb file with only a few layers—if those layers contain a lot of data—could easily become massive. To see how many tiles an image has, hold down the command while selecting the file size at the lower-left corner of the active file. Note that the number in the lower-left corner can reflect the flattened image size or the image size of the file with layers.

Photoshop compresses files that are saved in Photoshop format using a lossless compression called Run Length Encoding. Of course, a file with a minimum of image data in its layer tiles will compress more than a file whose layer tiles contain large amounts of data. And—for the same reason—highly complex tonal ranges covering the entire document won't compress as well as small flat tonal elements. Even with 3.0's compression scheme, layers will still eat up disk space but this will be a small price to pay. Like Composite Controls on steroids, layers should offer the kind of creative freedom you can drown in.

## New Tools & Commands

Quick Edit lets you acquire and work on a portion of a larger TIFF or Scitex file and then export it back into the original file.

The move tool lets you move selections, single and linked layers, and drag and drop between images.

The eraser tool can do its job with the airbrush, the paintbrush or the pencil—as well as the block that it was in 2.5. When you're working on a layer, you erase to transparency. When you work on the background, you erase to the background color.

The gradient tool can be set from foreground to transparent and vice versa. But this new option (to transparent) works only in layers because the background layer does not have transparency options. You can view the brush size of your painting tools by setting that option in the Preferences file. To access the elliptical marquee tool, just option-click the rectangular marquee tool.

The dodge/burn tool of old has become the dodge/burn/sponge tool. As in 2.5, you toggle between the tool options. The sponge tool increases/decreases saturation in the underlying image.

Gamut Warning checks the preferences in the monitor setup, printing inks setup and separation setup and displays in gray (or any other color specified in the Preferences window) the out-of-gamut colors based on the preferences. Gamut Warning alerts you to any colors in your image that are unprintable using the CMYK Gamut you set up in preferences.

The Replace Color and Color Range commands are a major enhancement in automatic selection over the magic wand. An especially useful feature of Color Range is the option of selecting all out-of-gamut colors and bringing them into gamut by desaturating them with either the sponge tool or the Hue/Saturation command. To avoid abrupt color changes, however, it's best to feather the selected areas before desaturating.

Preview CMYK shows onscreen—as accurately as an RGB monitor is capable of displaying CMYK colors—how those colors will print based on the color separation. This is useful when you must provide an image in RGB for later conversion to CMYK. Because you can work on your image in Preview CMYK mode, you can desaturate colors that are out of gamut to ensure more predictable color output.

Image Duplicate makes a copy of your image including all layers, layer masks and channels in a single-layer document. This allows you to make changes and to compare those changes to the unchanged original.

Save a Copy makes a new file with layers and channels without replacing the current file.

> **TIP: USING THE PATH TOOL**
> Judy L. Miller considers the path tool invaluable because it lets her outline things very accurately and provides a lot of control over elements; it's more accurate than the lasso tool. Once you've made a path, you can always use that path as a way to reload a selection without the large overhead of saving a channel. If you want to go back and make further adjustments to that path, you can do so by simply using the pen tool. Paths take up much less disk space than channels. Any saved path can also be made into a mask.

## Improved Interface

Photoshop 3.0's new drag-and-drop function allows very fluid image and layer selections: you can move a layer, selection or channel from one document to another without having to copy and paste.

Although displayed in groups, palettes can be repositioned, separated and customized by dragging a palette's tab. The Commands palette adds a button interface to function keys; you can customize it to fit your working needs by assigning key combinations to commands you use often and adding them to the palette.

You can also save file information with a file (File>Info) using the Newspaper Association of America (NAA) standard.

# Filters

A great convenience and timesaver is the Preview window, which is now part of all filter dialog boxes. This means, of course, that you can see how an effect will look on your image without having to actually apply it—and, more importantly, no more frustrating waits while Photoshop leisurely undoes an effect that didn't turn out quite the way you'd planned.

Lighting Effects allows up to 16 lights for which different light properties and types can be specified. The texture channel uses a grayscale texture to affect how the light appears to bounce off the surface of the image. You can choose a light's direction, color and other properties such as Material and Gloss. Lighting Effects is striking, but like many filters, you should use it subtly—and don't stick to the default settings.

The Clouds filter makes random cloud-like patterns using the foreground and background colors in the Tool palette. The Difference Clouds filter blends the foreground and background information with the pixels in the image. Reapplying this many times to the same selection results in drastically different displays of color.

The Dust and Scratches filter eliminates a radius of pixel noise based on the value entered in the dialog box.

If you're one of those fearless souls willing to delve into the mysteries of programming, Filter Factory (which ships on the accompanying CD) will provide ample opportunities to devise all those exciting filters you've only dreamed about. You can even put them on a disk and distribute them to others. To create a custom filter, you must use arithmetic expressions to determine how your filter will affect the channels of each pixel in an image. You can also add Settings dialog boxes with as many as eight sliders for altering the filter's effects. If you save the filter's expressions in a text file, you can go back and edit the file within Filter Factory.

> **TIP: USING THE MARQUEE**
> Richard Tuschman often uses the marquee selection tool with a feather, beginning with a 15-pixel radius, and saves it as a selection in an alpha channel, then pastes it into the file. If he doesn't like the level of feathering, instead of redoing the marquee selection with a different feather radius, he deletes it from the original file to leave that unchanged, then goes back to the alpha channel and starts experimenting until he gets the look he wants. If it's too soft, he'll adjust Levels to increase the contrast; if it's not soft enough, he'll apply the Gaussian Blur filter.

# Paths

To define a path as a clipping path, first save it, then choose Clipping Path from the Paths palette pop-up menu and designate the path and the flatness. You can also do this in the EPS dialog box; as long as the path is saved it doesn't have to be designated in the Paths palette option. However, you do have to specify the path in the EPS dialog box when saving it. If you save it as a clipping path in the Paths palette, it automatically fills in the path in the EPS dialog box. The option to save a path as a clipping path in the EPS dialog box almost fell by the wayside in 3.0, but it was added back because so many users wanted it. The even-odd fill rule and the non-zero winding fill options are gone. When saving in EPS format, you must designate the path in the EPS dialog box. To create a selection from a path, drag the path onto the selection icon at the bottom of the Paths palette. Double-click to save a work path or drag to the New Path option at the bottom of the palette.

## Selections

Under the Select menu, there are three new ways to affect a selection: Expand, Contract and Smooth. Expand adds a user-specified number of pixels; Contract removes pixels; and Smooth incorporates small pockets of small unselected pixels in the middle of a large selection to boost the continuity of the selection. Color Range allows you to select colors based on the range of colors you've determined. There are presets available for color ranges as well as for shadows, highlights and midtones. In addition, any color or multiple colors (shift>click) can be selected from either the preview or the image. There are multiple ways to preview the selection to best suit a user's needs, as Grayscale, White or Black mask, Quickmask or the original file. Fuzziness levels can be assigned and color ranges can be saved and loaded. You can alter selections with Remove Black Matte or Remove White Matte (Select>Matting). Similar to Defringe, these commands are typically used to get rid of glows or halos that surround pasted images.

Adobe very wisely built into Photoshop 3.0 many of the best functions to be found in the competition. Artists at all levels should eagerly anticipate trying out these new tools. Although you may find yourself thinking you could do many of the same functions in the previous version, most of them are much easier now.

Mitchell Hartman, an artist based in North White Plains, New York, discovered an interesting technique for producing either an emboss or paper-texture effect in Photoshop 3.0. With an image file open, choose Lighting Effect (Filter>Render). In the subsequent dialog box you'll see a preview of your image with an oval representing the area to be lighted. Change the default settings: Light Type from Spotlight to Omni (the direction of the light). The oval over the picture turns to a circle. Click on any point in the circle to encompass the entire image.

Next double-click the yellow box to bring up the Color palette and choose a color for this effect (the paler the better). As you move the intensity slider, watch the preview image to see how much light is actually hitting the image.

In the Properties window, set Gloss to Shiny (about 54), Material to Metallic (54) and Exposure (about 8) (again experiment while watching the image). Leave Ambiance at 0 and change the color box again to the pale color you chose earlier.

In the Texture Channel dialog box, change None to Green. This selects the highlight channel, which is necessary because embossing reverses the content of the channel. Therefore, the highlight reverses to a shadow, which is the effect you want to use for the emboss "bump." Click the "White is high" box and move the slider to Mountainous (about 65), then click OK and you're done.

To produce the kind of paper texture effect you'd get in Fractal Design Painter or PixelPaint Pro 3, follow the same process just described for the emboss effect except that before you apply the Lighting Effects filter, you must create an alpha channel (Channel 4). In that channel add a texture such as a noise pattern and invert it, so that when you apply the emboss effect, the pattern will revert back to its original form. In the Lighting Effects filter dialog box, use Channel 4 as the texture channel and your texture will be applied with the lighting effect.

Normal image (left) and embossed image.

**Artist:** Annabelle Breakey
**Image:** Sea Life
**Software:** Photoshop 3.0; Kai's Power Tools 2.0;
Gallery Effects, Classic Art, Vol. 2

Like Bert Monroy's *Akihabara* image described later in this chapter—Annabelle Breakey's whimsical image, *Sea Life*, consists of no scanned images; it was entirely computer generated. Its style, though, is entirely different than Monroy's photorealistic imagery, which shows just how much digitally generated artwork can vary from artist to artist. Breakey, a San Francisco-based photo-illustrator, has discovered some dramatic effects, which she's used in *Sea Life*, most notably her own customized emboss effect. Unlike Photoshop's, it doesn't obliterate the embossed object's color. Although she could have used layers to create this image, she chose to use channels instead, both to save disk space and to generate some interesting effects.

**TIP: A QUICK WAY TO CLEAN UP A SELECTION**
When you have an active selection that's been cut from a white background and pasted over another image, you'll often get an outline of white pixels. You can eliminate that outline on the Layers palette by moving the right slider for the floating selection from 255 to approximately 250.

For this image, done for a stock photo collection, she began by generating a blue-green background with KPT's Texture Explorer. The closest she came to using a scanned image was a digital photo of an anchor, which she pasted into a channel and loaded into the image. Then she colorized the selection using the Hue/Saturation sliders, which gave the anchor a translucent look.

To create the embossed effect of the nautilus shell, Breakey devised her own version of an emboss filter, because she wanted more control—specifically, color control—than Photoshop's Emboss filter provides. She pasted the shell into a channel filled with black, made a pen tool path around the outside edge of the shell and saved the path. Back in the channel she selected all, then pressed the up arrow twice and the left arrow twice.

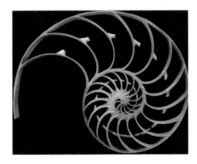

Original channel of the shell.

After loading the selection (the shell) in the RGB channel, she went to the Paths palette and selected the shell path and the Make Selection command.

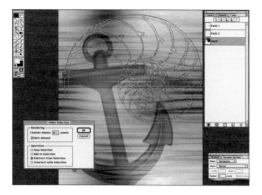

Loaded channel with pen tool path and Make Selection dialog box (with Subtract chosen).

In the resulting dialog box, she set a Feather Radius of 0 and subtracted from the loaded selection to create the selection for the top (to be highlighted) edge of the shell.

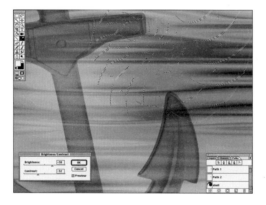

Brightness/Contrast dialog box with top (highlighted) edge.

Then, in the Brightness/Contrast dialog box, she set Brightness to +38 and Contrast to -32. Once she'd deselected the highlighted area, she went back to the original channel and selected all again. Then she pressed the down arrow four times and the right arrow four times (two pixels to get back to the original position, then two more). Back in the RGB channel, Breakey loaded the selection, and again in the Paths palette's Make Selection dialog box, subtracted from the selection to make the bottom (shadow) edge.

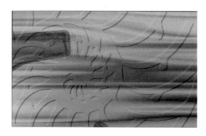

Detail of bottom (shadow) edge.

In the Brightness/Contrast dialog box, she set the Brightness to -68. Going back to the shell's original path, she made that into a new selection, then changed Brightness to -28 and Contrast to +47.

Detail of finished embossed shell.

The fish were drawn in a channel with the pen tool so they could be loaded later into the image. To make a fuzzy medium-gray line around the pen tool path, Breakey stroked the path with the airbrush tool with Brush Options of 16-pixel Diameter, 0 percent Hardness, 25 percent Spacing and pressure sensitivity set to 70 percent (this last option is only available with a pressure-sensitive tablet).

The fuzzy stroked path.

To make the dotted line, she used the airbrush (at 100 percent pressure) with a lighter shade of gray, Brush Options at 5-pixel Diameter, 0 percent Hardness and 100 percent Spacing.

The dotted stroked path.

The bright dotted stroked path over the soft, fuzzy stroked path provided a neon glow that she used in the final image. Then in the RGB channel, Breakey loaded the fish selection, and in Levels, she changed the colors of the loaded selection and deselected it. Going back to the channel, she drew an imprecise path around the fish and saved that. In the RGB channel, she made the path into a selection with a four-pixel feather and inverted the colors.

Detail of the two paths combined to create the neon glow.

Detail of the finished fish.

The scallop shell began as a drawing made with the pen tool in a channel; Breakey stroked the path with a white fuzzy airbrush (2 percent pressure), 19-pixel Diameter, 0 percent Hardness, 1 percent Spacing. Then she stroked the path again, this time with Brush Options of 2-pixel Diameter, 0 percent Hardness and 1 percent Spacing.

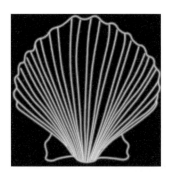

The original scallop channel.

Copying the scallop channel, she pasted it into a new channel and applied Gaussian Blur set to 15. Back in the RGB channel, she loaded the blurred scallop selection, set Brightness to +100 and repeated that two more times.

The blurred scallop channel.

In Color Balance, she changed Shadows, Midtones and Highlights to make the soft white glow yellow, and deselected. After loading the original scallop channel, she applied the KPT Grime Layer to get a sandy, speckled effect. Finally, in Color Balance, she changed the color to dark blue.

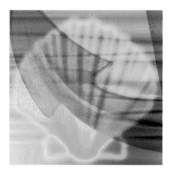

Detail of yellow shell.

Detail of final shell.

**Artist:** Don Day
**Image:** Memory Woods 2
**Software:** Photoshop 3.0

For this image, Day began by colorizing a black-and-white photo of trees in the woods. After adjusting the Curves to add contrast, he switched from Grayscale to RGB mode, then used the Colorize option in Hue/Saturation, setting the green hue to about 162. In the Curves dialog box, he exaggerated the curves in the RGB channel as well as separately in the red, green and blue channels. The resulting image he posterized to eight levels.

To create the fire inside the hand, he used Color Range to isolate the color photo of the hand from the black background, then saved the selection. Using Color Range again, he selected the hand's midtones and highlights, then used the same "crazy curves" technique to colorize the hand image. Copying the fire image on a dark background, he pasted it into the selected area of the hand and positioned it for the best "fire-in-hand" effect. After loading the selection, he dragged it to the background image to make it a floating selection. He then dragged it to the Layer icon to make it a new layer.

**TIP: SMOOTH RGB-TO-CMYK CONVERSIONS**
To get smooth transitions between RGB and CMYK color, Judy L. Miller uses the TrueMatch color system with swatch book. The system is built into Photoshop. You can buy the swatch book directly from TrueMatch Corporation (331 Madison Ave., NY 10017; 212/351-2360) or through graphic design mail-order firms.

To make the triangular blend, Day first created a new layer. Copying the fire-in-hand image to the Clipboard, he drew a triangle with the pen tool, made it a selection and saved it to a channel. There he created a top-to-bottom gradation. He loaded the selection, filled it with magenta and pasted the hand image into the triangular gradient selection, on top of the existing hand image. Next he duplicated the triangle selection and saved it to a new channel, where he created a bottom-to-top gradient in the triangle. After loading that selection, he changed the foreground color to black and option-deleted to fill it. Finally, he used Levels to taper off the gradient.

**Artist:** Bert Monroy
**Image:** Akihabara
**Software:** Photoshop 3.0; Illustrator 5.5

Bert Monroy is a Bay area artist who specializes in photorealism. All his images look like they could be photographs but in fact they're entirely computer-generated. Because his images generally consist of so many elements, he has found Photoshop 3.0's Layers especially appealing. With Layers, he can quickly and easily place different elements into an image, manipulating and rearranging as often as necessary without integrating into the finished art until he's satisfied with the result.

For this image, Monroy drew many of the elements in Illustrator and brought them into Photoshop. Once these elements were placed, they had to be arranged on the shelves in much the same way that actual products are placed on store shelves. During the positioning process, Monroy found that rearranging some of the items resulted in a more realistic, balanced look.

To create the shelves stocked with telephones in the center of the image, Monroy began by making one phone in Illustrator, which he subsequently used to generate all the others.

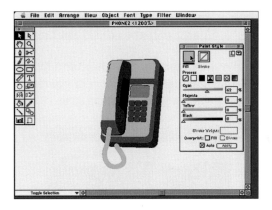

The original phone created in Illustrator.

Monroy uses Illustrator because it lets him quickly create an object that he can copy and modify to make different versions of the original. After drawing the original phone, he made various changes to the duplicates such as changing the color, repositioning the buttons, adding buttons and changing the arrangement of the cord.

Several duplicates of the phone after they were modified and were waiting to go on the shelf.

Once 32 phones were completed, Monroy placed them into individual layers in the Photoshop file.

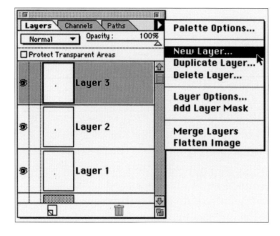

The Layers palette with a layer selected.

As with channels, effects can be applied to layers. There—using the dodge/burn/sponge and airbrush tools and the Add Noise filter—he added the lighting and texture effects that gave the phones their realistic look.

Each phone was then arranged on the shelf and scaled to add the effect of perspective. Once all the phones were correctly positioned, the layers were merged into the overall image.

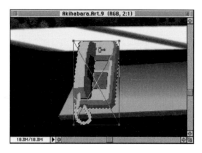

One of the phones after it was retouched.

One of the phones placed on the shelf.

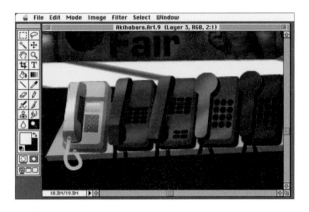

The phones arranged on the shelf.

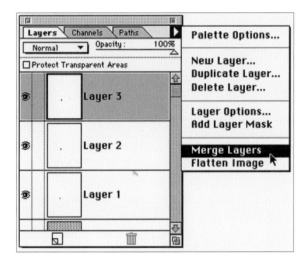

Merging the layers into one.

The finished shelf with all the merchandise neatly arranged.

**Artist:** Wendy Grossman
**Image:** Educational Record
**Software:** Photoshop 3.0; Illustrator 5.5; Adobe
Dimensions 1.0; Ray Dream Designer 3.0; Gallery
Effects, Vols. 1, 2 and 3; Kai's Power Tools 2.0

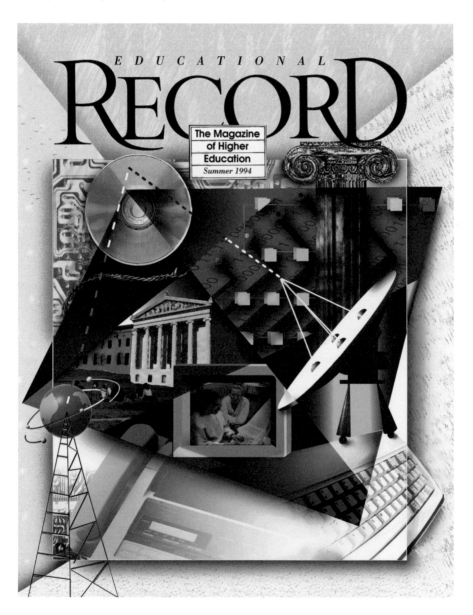

Wendy Grossman is an artist and illustrator based in New York City. This image was designed as a magazine cover for *Educational Record*, published by the Department of Education in Washington, D.C., to illustrate a story about how the information superhighway will affect higher education.

Grossman started with a pencil sketch, which she scanned into Photoshop and opened in Illustrator. There, she determined the correct sizes, shapes and colors of all the elements. All the elements (such as the purple circuit board, the yellow boxes on the circuit board and the binary numbers) were built as separate Illustrator files and brought into the main image as they were created. Grossman uses Illustrator for this because it provides more control in creating graphic images.

The original pencil sketch.

Once the Illustrator file was complete, she opened it in Photoshop and brought in the base of the column (created in Ray Dream Designer), adding it to the background layer. The column itself was a scanned photo she added to the base. Next she brought in the fax machine (a scan of a black-and-white photo) on its own layer.

Then she added a layer mask and used the gradient tool to create a transparent blend (black-to-white linear blend with a 50 midpoint skew) to be applied to the fax machine. At that point, she made it a shade of magenta.

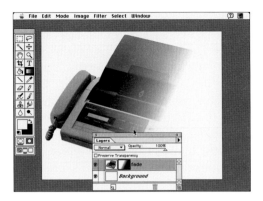

The mask for the fax machine layer with a gradient blend applied and the background layer turned off.

After drawing the satellite dish in Photoshop and modeling its legs in Ray Dream Designer, Grossman put them on a new layer and added the scanned CD to another layer. The satellite's legs looked too flat, so to make them look more three-dimensional, Grossman applied Photoshop's new Lighting Effects filter to them, using a yellow spotlight.

The image after the mask was applied and the satellite layer and the CD layer were added.

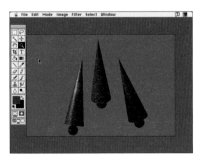

The satellite legs before the Lighting Effects filter was applied.

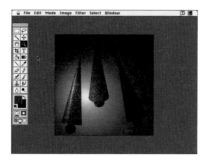

The satellite legs after the Lighting Effects filter was applied.

After scanning the CD, she used Levels and Curves to manipulate the colors, then brought it into the document on a layer and specified a blending mode, Hard Light, at 100 percent opacity. Unfortunately, Hard Light mode made the fingerprints on the scanned CD very apparent. To remove them, Grossman made a new layer and set the opacity to 100 percent in Normal mode. Using the rubber stamp tool to clone a similar area around the fingerprints, she checked the Sample Merged option to make the tool pick up all the layers underneath the active layer and clone them onto the active layer.

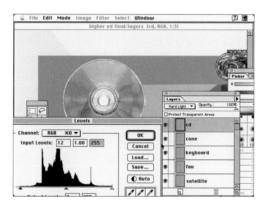

The CD layer with the shadows being deepened using the Levels command.

The buildings and people were composited from two different scans; after colorizing them, she applied the Gallery Effects filter Dry Brush.

Inverting the original scan of the circuit board from yellow to blue, Grossman copied it to the Clipboard. After creating a new layer (named Back), she made a path with the pen tool, made it into a selection, then pasted the circuit board into the selection. She scaled it and changed the colors using Levels and Color Balance. Repeating this process with the rest of the background resulted in different shapes in slightly different colors.

The question mark was done in Dimensions and saved as an Illustrator file. Grossman made a new layer (called Quest) and used the Place command to add the question mark. In an alpha channel, she made a drop shadow for it.

To make the tassel, she scanned a black-and-white photo and flipped and rotated it to get it in the right position.

The image after the tassel and the question mark layers were added.

She then colorized the tassel and copied it to the Clipboard. Next she created a new layer (called Tassel) and pasted the tassel into it. To create the illusion of the tassel wrapping around the button, she selected the top part of the tassel and rotated it into the proper position to make it appear to wrap around the button.

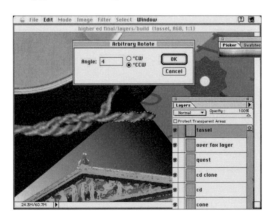

In the tassel layer, a portion of the tassel was selected and rotated into place.

In Photoshop, she made a low-res EPS file for placement only and opened the EPS file in Illustrator so she could precisely position the dots. To create the dots, she went back to Illustrator. After clicking the Stroke box in the Paint Styles palette, she used the

Dashed option in the Line dialog box to adjust the spaces between the dots. She saved the dots as a separate file and placed it in the Photoshop document on a new layer.

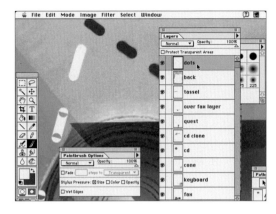

The dots layer being added to the image.

This is where Layers really made a difference. After Grossman submitted the finished image, her client decided she wanted some elements changed: the question mark and the shadow over the fax machine had to be removed; the background was to be redone. Because she had not yet flattened the image, Grossman simply went back to those layers and made the changes. What could have taken an extra three hours of work was done in about three minutes.

The image after the background, the question mark and the shadow layers were removed.

**Artist:** Wendy Grossman
**Image:** India
**Software**: Photoshop 3.0; Adobe Illustrator 5.5;
Ray Dream Designer 3.0; Adobe Dimensions 1.0;
Gallery Effects, Vols. 1, 2 and 3

This image was created to use in a demonstration of alternative printing processes at Siggraph 1994. It was printed on silk and also on cornhusk papyrus.

Grossman began by scanning a sketch of the whole illustration into Photoshop, saved it as a PICT file and imported it into Illustrator where she used it as a template.

In Ray Dream Designer, she created the more complex palm trees; the simple lotus blossoms she made in Dimensions.

Back in Photoshop, she began adding various elements and made a separate layer for the deities. She scanned in a postcard depicting the Indian goddess Laksmi and saved it as Laksmi. Then she applied a Gallery Effects filter called Plaster and saved the result of that as a file called Laksmi Plaster.

The Illustrator file opened in Photoshop after several background elements were added.

The figure of the goddess Laksmi with the GE Plaster filter being applied.

She went back to the original scanned postcard and pasted into it a copy of Laksmi Plaster using 61 percent opacity in Normal mode.

The Plaster-filtered image being pasted into the original image.

She then deselected it. Still in the Laksmi file, she duplicated its background layer. This enabled her to delete the original background layer using the delete layer command and place another layer underneath the background. She created a layer of white (Layer 1) and composited that underneath the background, setting the opacity to 100 percent in Normal mode.

The background copy being composited with the white layer underneath it.

In the Layer Options dialog box, she moved the white triangle for the active layer ("This Layer") to 211. This allowed some of the pixels from the underlying layer (the white layer) to show through the top layer. Grossman used this technique with all the deities in the circle.

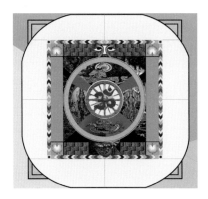

After all four deities were added to the circle using the same compositing techniques.

Next she used Photoshop 3.0's new Color Range command to select the sky, with Quick Mask as the selection preview option. This displayed everything that wasn't selected as red. Next she applied the Cloud filter to the sky. Then she inversed the selection to select the man practicing yoga. Applying the Gallery Effects Dry Brush filter (Brush Size 2; Brush Detail 9; Texture 2) to the figure gave it a painterly effect. Once all the male figures were placed, she used the GE Craquelure filter (Crack Spacing 56; Crack Depth 7; Crack Brightness 7) on all of them.

The sky being selected with the Color Range command using the Quick Mask preview mode (red areas are not selected).

To clean up the center circle, Grossman first selected it with the elliptical marquee. Since her selection was a few pixels too large, she used Photoshop 3.0's new Contract command (Select>Modify) to decrease the selection by two pixels while keeping it in the proper proportions; without this handy tool, she would have had to redo the selection. Finally, to isolate a layer that needed additional work, she hid all the other layers and made only the active layer visible.

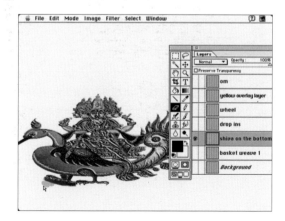

After all the layers except the active one were made invisible, to simplify cleanup of the active layer.

**Artist:** Greg Vander Houwen
**Image:** Tunnel Vision
**Software:** Photoshop 3.0

Greg Vander Houwen is an artist and illustrator based in the Seattle area. For this image, he started with two scanned photos, one of clouds, the other trees.

The sky on the background layer.

To add a color emboss effect to the clouds, he first selected all, floated the selection and applied Photoshop's Emboss filter; then in the Layers palette, he set the mode to Luminosity and the opacity to about 60 percent. After defloating the selection and adjusting the colors with the Hue/Saturation command, Vander Houwen floated the image again but this time in Difference mode. Because he wanted to affect only the highlights of the clouds, he moved the Blend sliders in Layer Options until he got the effect he wanted—darkening the highlights to produce a solarize effect. (Using Difference mode also produced a blending effect.) Then he inverted the map, resulting in an eerie-looking sky, which he saved as a separate file.

The sky after it was embossed.

The sky after it was inverted.

The original trees scan.

He created the orchard element by extracting masks from what-ever channels offered the most contrast in the areas he wanted to effect. To isolate and brighten the sky, he used the sky mask.

The sky mask.

After generating a mask from the trees image, he loaded it as a selection to isolate the trees and offset them slightly. At that point, Vander Houwen floated the selection and color-embossed it. Both the sky and the tree masks were used to enhance and select areas of the tree scan; then that selection was duplicated and saved to a separate layer.

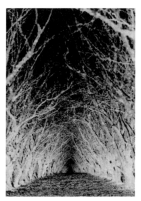

The trees mask.

With the selection still floating, he dragged its layer name onto the Make Layer icon to put it on a new layer. In the Layer Options dialog box, he held down the option key to split the slider triangles just enough to feather the effect into the underlying image. The final step for this element was to build a border. Using the magic wand with Tolerance set to about 20, he selected the border area, feathered it a couple of pixels, inverted and saved the selection. That meant he could use it to select just the interior of the image, which he could then duplicate and put on a new layer in the inverted sky file he'd previously saved. In the Layer Options dialog box, he set the opacity to about 90 percent and moved the white triangle of that layer's Blend slider to the light gray part of the bar to make all the light areas transparent. Holding down the option key, he split the slider again to feather the effect.

The edge selection.

To make the sky and trees appear to be intertwined, he duplicated the background layer (the inverted sky) and saved it to a new layer. He offset it a couple of pixels and then used Layer Options to apply a difference setting to the underlying images, the inverted sky and the trees element.

The sky and trees layered.

The sky and trees layers after Difference was applied.

The third element was the tunnel. To resize and distort it so that it would fit the shape of the orchard row, he placed the image into its own layer in the main file, set opacity in Layer Options to roughly 50 percent and distorted the tunnel until it fit. Setting the tunnel layer to be semitransparent allowed him to see how the tunnel distortions would relate to the underlying images. When he was satisfied with the distortion effect, he painted black over the areas of the tunnel image he wanted to disappear. Then in Layer Options he boosted the opacity to about 90 percent and moved the black triangle on that layer's Blend slider to a midtone gray, which made all the black areas transparent.

The original tunnel
image.

The tunnel after it
was distorted.

To feather the effect, he held down the option key and again split
the slider. To further integrate the tunnel with the rest of the image,
he set the rubber stamp tool to clone from saved and then selected a
soft-edged brush and set it to about 70 percent opacity. Now he
could simply paint away the parts of the tunnel he didn't want to
the underlying saved image.

The sky, trees and tunnel
composited.

**Artist:** David Teich
**Image:** Domestic Violence
**Software:** Photoshop 3.0

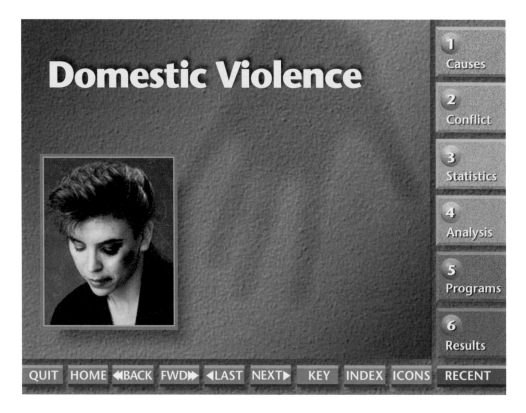

David Teich is an artist and illustrator who lives and works in Roosevelt, New Jersey. This image was done as part of an interactive CD-ROM project that dealt with domestic violence issues. It was designed to have six chapters, each dealing with a different aspect of the topic, and all tied together with a unified appearance.

The background layer was a simple texture created in Photoshop by applying the Noise filter (with the Monochromatic box checked and Amount set to 99), Gaussian Blur 1, Emboss and Hue/Saturation.

The background layer.

The main panel in the upper left (a copy of the noise background) he put on a separate layer, adding another layer (Big Box Shadow) between it and the background layer. Consisting of a simple feathered selection filled with 50 percent black, it was used as a drop shadow for the main panel.

Layer 1: Big Box Shadow

Teich put each chapter's buttons on a layer of their own and linked them; he did the same with their drop shadows. He created the first chapter button within a rectangular selection using the Add Noise filter and with the lasso tool selected areas as bevels and gave them highlights or shadows with Curves. He then duplicated the first button five times and changed each one's color.

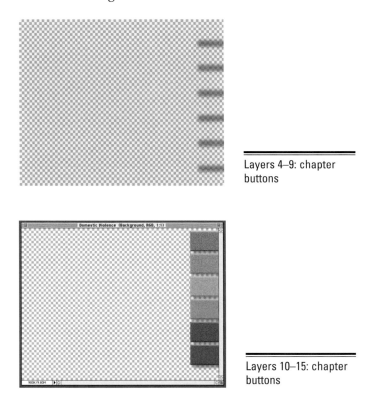

Layers 4–9: chapter buttons

Layers 10–15: chapter buttons

The round chapter number buttons were round selections with the KPT Glass Lens Bright filter applied. Teich set their layer to Luminosity to maintain the background color of each.

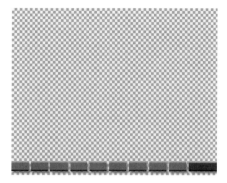

Navigators and
Navigator's shadow
buttons.

The universal navigation buttons along the bottom of the screen he created on one layer, putting their associated drop shadows on another layer beneath theirs. The photo box, which varies in size and color from one screen to another, was on its own layer, as was its drop shadow. On this layer, Teich also added a gradation from the large panel box to the photo, designed to draw attention to the photo.

The shadow layer for
the photo box.

Text and text shadows were created for various screens and put on upper layers. He applied the Navigator's Shadow, Photo Box Shadow and Text Shadow in Multiply mode to darken areas beneath them.

Text and shadow with the Navigator.

To create the shadow of an attacker's hand on the wall behind the victim's face, Teich traced his own hand and scanned it. He filled the outine, blurred it, then set its layer options to a 40 percent Soft Light. Compositing it against the background texture produced a subtle but frightening image.

Many of these elements could have been created on a single layer, to save memory and storage space. But developing this project required maximum flexibility, making the use of numerous layers essential. f/x

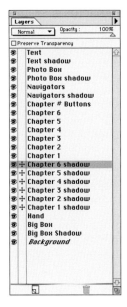

All the layers listed in the Layers palette.

# CHAPTER 2

# Photoshop f/x:
# Special Effects With Third-Party Filters

Anyone who's used Photoshop for very long knows that the program comes with a variety of useful filters for manipulating images. Many people are quite content to use only native Photoshop filters; others shy away from third-party plug-ins because they tend to produce effects that look too wild or obviously computer-generated. It's often easy to spot an image that's been affected by certain filters since their out-of-the-box settings are likely to produce recognizable results.

However, if you're willing to take some time and experiment—and accept the fact that you may wind up with only one or two really superb effects for every ten or twenty throw-aways, you may find that you're able to produce some striking filtered images that don't look like everyone else's. Below are general descriptions of some of the better-known and most interesting effects generators. This is not intended to be an exhaustive list; just an indication of what types of filters are out there and some of the effects you can produce with them. Beyond that are a number of images produced by some talented artists to which they've applied a variety of filters—sometimes in conjunction with native Photoshop filters—always creatively.

# Gallery Effects, Volumes 1, 2 and 3

## Adobe Systems

Each Gallery Effects volume consists of 16 different filters, many of them similar to native Photoshop filters. All the filters contain a preview window that lets you see the effect of applying that filter by applying it to a small section of your image. Volume 1 includes a number of natural-media effects, including Watercolor, Graphic Pen, Chalk and Charcoal, Fresco and Dry Brush. The GE Emboss filter, unlike Photoshop's Emboss filter, preserves the colors in your image.

Volume 2 filters let you simulate particular painting and drawing techniques—such as Rough Pastels, Angled Strokes, Palette Knife and Colored Pencil—as well as photographic and texture effects like Glowing Edges, Bas Relief, Grain and Photocopy.

Some of the unusual filters in Volume 3 that can produce dramatic effects are Plastic Wrap, Cutout and Plaster. Others include Stained Glass, Sponge, Torn Edges and Water Paper.

# Paint Alchemy

## Xaos Tools

Paint Alchemy, a streamlined version of Pandemonium, Xaos's image-processing/animation software for Silicon Graphics workstations, is actually one all-encompassing filter that comes with 76 predefined styles and 36 brushes. From that stepping-off point, you can move into uncharted territory, creating and applying an endless variety of special-effect brush strokes to selected areas of an image.

Each style can be completely customized with 30 controls within five Control Cards—Brush, Color, Size, Angle and Transparency. If that's not enough control for you, Paint Alchemy lets you create your own brushes from any PICT file. You can even define control settings relative to an image's attributes—such as using an image's hue, saturation or brightness to vary a brush's size, angle or opacity. Controls include density, jitter, layering variations, hue, saturation and brightness. An optional disk of 50 additional brushes (Floppy Full of Brushes) is also available.

# Terrazzo

## Xaos Tools

Terrazzo lets you create kaleidoscopic repeating patterns from any PICT or Photoshop image in RGB, CMYK and Grayscale modes.

Using any of 17 symmetries to create and tile a geometric pattern, you can produce dramatically different patterns just by moving the symmetrical shape you've selected to different areas of your image. Once you've settled on a pattern, you can alter its opacity, lightness, darkness, hue, saturation and brightness. Continuous Preview lets you see and fine-tune patterns as you create them. Blend Radius lets you blur tile edges to minimize the tiling effect. You can also make Terrazzo tiles uniquely your own by applying other filters to them.

> **TIP: SELECTIVE UNDO FOR FILTERING IN PHOTOSHOP**
> Mark Landman has found that you can achieve the same effect as Fractal Design Painter's Fade command, which lets you undo your last operation by a user-specified percentage. By applying a filter to a floating selection or a layer and changing its opacity on the Layers palette, you can selectively undo an effect that's too intense for a subtler result.

# Kai's Power Tools

## HSC Software

Kai's Power Tools (KPT) comes with 37 filters—some are variations of native Photoshop filters, while others are strikingly different but easily recognizable as KPT filters, unless you devise subtle techniques for achieving your own customized effects.

Probably the best known and most popular KPT filters are Gradient Designer, Texture Explorer and Fractal Explorer. With Gradient Designer you can apply multicolor gradations to a selection or just along its edge. A gradient can have an unlimited number of colors and numerous transparency levels, for fading in and out of an image. Texture Explorer lets you mathematically generate endlessly tiling patterns. You can even generate textures from colors in a saved gradation. Fractal Explorer includes one Mandelbrot and three Julia set explorers for your fractal-creating pleasure. Just as with Texture Explorer, you can apply colors from saved gradations. Fractal Explorer provides numerous controls, including the ability to adjust the amount of detail, zoom in on previews and alter spiral and radial wrapping.

Other filters include Vortex Tiling, which tiles an image in a spiral pattern; and Glass Lens, which gives images a spherelike quality.

**Artist:** Kai Krause
**Image:** Cathedral Window
**Software:** Photoshop 3.0; Kai's Power Tools 2.1

With this image, Krause was trying to convey the look of stained glass by using vivid, high-contrast colors in what's known as a negative rainbow—spectral colors with inverted hue settings, as found in polarized crystals and oil slicks.

Using the Difference mode of KPT's Gradient Designer, he added six layers of gradients sweeping around in 360 degrees (an algorithm not offered by Photoshop, which has only linear and circular). Each one has a complex spectrum of colors designed within the Gradient Designer (and saved for future use) and is then applied to the image. Where the gradient is white, it turns the color underneath to its opposite; where it's black it won't affect the underlying image. Shades of gray reverse the color gradually.

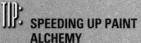

**SPEEDING UP PAINT ALCHEMY**
Here's how Mark Landman solves a performance problem that's specific to Paint Alchemy: when you have numerous items in the Plug-ins folder, Paint Alchemy's performance slows to a crawl. That's because every time you use it, it scans all the filters in the folder. Simply pull Paint Alchemy out of the folder and replace it with an alias, and the problem instantly disappears.

The frame around the window was created inside Gradient Designer as well—a rectangle fill gradient consisting of 90 percent of clear nothingness, and a little sharp black area.

**Artist:** Mark Jasin
**Image:** Mariah Carey
**Software:** Photoshop; Gallery Effects, Vol. 1

This image was one of a series of music star photo-illustrations commissioned by Wherehouse Records to be silkscreened onto large posters. For this reason, Jasin intentionally output them at low (130 dpi) resolution. Because he had to work with a wide variety of pho-

tos provided by the client—some were halftones, some were color; some were high quality and others were very poor—and they all had to look fairly consistent, Jasin decided the best solution was to turn them all into duotones and cover up their differences with an arsenal of filters.

Scanning a black-and-white photo of singer Mariah Carey, Jasin converted it to Duotone mode, choosing a dark indigo blue and a pale lavender. Once he'd done that, he began selecting different areas and applying different filters to them. He used Gallery Effects's Spatter filter and Watercolor filter in the upper-left corner; selecting other areas, he

**TIP: AVOIDING OUT-OF-MEMORY PROBLEMS**
If you're using a filter and you get an out-of-memory error message, Don Day suggests using the filter on an individual channel rather than the entire image. If that doesn't work, as a last resort try using the Piggy Plug-in by taking it out of the Optional Extensions folder and putting it in the Plug-ins folder. But be prepared for a performance hit. Because the Piggy Plug-in disables the Photoshop memory management system, it can slow Photoshop to a crawl.

dropped out whites or blacks, then changed Curves and Levels. On the singer's right hand he used the Diffuse filter (Stylize menu); on her left hand he applied Mosaic. Noise was used in various places at various amounts; Gallery Effects's Watercolor and Spatter filters as well as Photoshop's Facet and Mosaic filters can be seen on the upper-right corner; he used Mosaic again in the upper-right area, but at a finer setting than he'd used on the hand.

# Andromeda Filters, Series 1, 2 and 3

## Andromeda Software

Series 1 Photography Filters is a set of ten filters that lets you create effects such as repeating vector patterns, starburst highlights and repeating images that rotate inside a circular grid. The Designs filter includes a mezzo screen option. Other filters include variations on Photoshop's Motion Blur and Lens Flare effects.

Series 2 3D Filter lets you wrap and rotate an image around any of four three-dimensional forms—a sphere, a box, a cylinder or a 2D plane floating in 3D space. You can spin, scale or rotate the 3D object and its surface. You can add a light source and change its position and orientation to shade the surface and the image on the surface, view the surface from any viewing angle and perspective and see an accurate preview rendering in the Preview window.

Series 3 Mezzo Filter provides mezzo screening, an alternative to conventional halftone dot screening for an illustrated effect. This filter outputs black-and-white line art derived from a grayscale Photoshop image. You can convert a grayscale image to a mezzotint or a mezzo-line—or you can design your own custom mezzo screen.

The Mezzogram feature heightens image detail and black-and-white contrast.

# FotoMagic

## Ring of Fire

This set of nine filters produces a variety of photographic effects. ColorExpander controls the gamut (number of colors) of an image; ColorFilters lets you selectively brighten or darken a color or color range; ColorNoise lets you add noise within a specified color range for randomizing colors; ColorRanger divides an image into eight colorized ranges to produce multichromatic effects, while ColorRanger II allows you to create multichannel duotone-like images. It accepts up to 256 colors simultaneously and lets you blend between colors to provide soft transitions. Both ColorRanger and ColorRanger II convert colors based on their luminosity instead of their hue. ColorReversal converts negative film into a positive image with highlight, shadow and exposure control. ColorFilters simulates a traditional photographic lens; it auto-compensates for adding and subtracting colors simultaneously. ColorScaler can quickly make any selection in an RGB image grayscale or simulate a duotone in any color.

# Alien Skin

## Virtus Corporation

This new texture generator is both a Photoshop plug-in and a stand-alone application. (It's no coincidence that this product has the same name as the company that makes The Black Box filters; it was developed by Alien Skin, the company, but is being marketed by Virtus.) Unlike Xaos Tools's Terrazzo, which lets you create patterns from any PICT image you supply, Alien Skin generates textures and terrains through mathematical mutations. Therefore, it works only with the mathematically defined textures supplied with the program (about 500 are expected).

Alien Skin produces resolution-independent texture tiles, in either RGB or CMYK mode, that can be scaled to any size or aspect ratio. To create a new texture, you select one of the presets, move a slider to set the Mutation rate and press the Mutate button. You'll get 12 new tiles, each a different variation of the original, plus you can "mate" two existing texture tiles to produce even more unusual "offspring." Alien Skin lets you generate height maps for 3D textures; it also supports transparency, lighten and darken modes.

# The Black Box

## Alien Skin Software

This six-filter set generates interesting effects in and around the borders of selected areas. Filters include Drop Shadow, Glow and an embossing filter aptly named The Boss. Swirl distorts images into whirlpool patterns, while Glass makes your image look like you've laid a sheet of glass on top of it; you can bevel the edges and change the refraction level. HSB Noise gets its name by allowing you to individually edit the hue, saturation and brightness levels of the images you apply it to.

There's one slight complication involving these filters, though. Because they're applied to the outer edge of a selection rather than the selection itself, they deselect the area that was originally selected. As a result, you must save the original or a snapshot before applying a filter and then revert to the saved version in order to composite the filtered image with the original.

**Artist:** Jim Allman
**Image:** Babyface
**Software:** Photoshop 3.0; The Black Box

## Simulating paper cutouts with The Black Box

Here's how you can use filters to take scanned drawings into Photoshop, trim the excess "paper" from their edges and layer them over a Photoshop background. Then you can use The Black Box's Drop Shadow filter—as Jim Allman did in *Babyface*—to create the effect of paper "cutouts" hanging in front of the background—such as multiple colored lights—as shown here. (Drop Shadow currently works only on "flat" files or in the background layer of a multilayer image.)

There should be a visual logic to the placement of shadows, so that objects intended to be in the foreground cast longer and fuzzier shadows.

Begin by scanning drawings in grayscale at 600 ppi. Then create a blank background image and fill it with light gray. Apply HSB Noise (Hue = 5, Saturation = 10, Brightness = 30) to make it a speckled gray. Select all, float it and fill with a bright color in Saturation mode; this increases the overall saturation of the background, turning it into bright multicolored speckles.

To make the background texture, use the Swirl filter (Whirlpool Spacing = 36, Smear Length = 10, Twist = 60, Streak Detail = 40, Warp = Off). Copy the scanned images from another document and paste them onto the background. Keep them floating while you scale them, position them on the background, adjust Curves to "bleach" the paper white at the edges and use the Command key and the magic wand tool (Tolerance = 30) to deselect the outer paper edges of the drawing. Save the new selection (which should closely follow the outline of the drawing) for future use, then defloat the selection.

After you've placed all your drawings and saved their boundaries into alpha channels, just load each selection in turn and generate drop shadows to suggest the desired light sources. Remember that objects that are farther from the background should cast longer shadows (set higher X Offset and Y Offset values in the Drop Shadow dialog box), and their shadows should have more feathered edges (a higher Blur value in Drop Shadow). Typical values in this image were: X Offset = 25 pixels, Y Offset = -33 pixels, Blur = 8 pixels, Opacity = 20 percent.

# Creating Your Own Effects

The most successful applications of filters are those that are subtly crafted from successive passes of the same filter, combinations of different filters, applications of filters to individual layers or channels and other innovative techniques. The artists whose images appear in this chapter and throughout the book can certainly attest to that. The striking effects they've managed to produce should inspire you to launch your own experiments with whatever filter collections you find appealing.

If you're looking for an effect that stands out from the rest, don't apply a filter to your entire image, as most people do. Try this alternative from Diane Fenster: duplicate the image, posterize the duplicate, make a selection with the magic wand and feather the selection, then apply the filter to the selection. (Since posterizing reduces the number of colors in an image, it's easier to make selections with the magic wand because so much more of the image gets selected—and you usually end up with interesting, irregularly shaped selections.) After you've applied the filter, copy it and place it on a new layer over the original image. Using various blending modes and opacities, you can achieve many different kinds of effects—much more than you'd ever get from applying the filter to the original image alone.

> **TIP: MAKING 3D TERRAZZO PATTERNS**
>
> Xaos Tools's Terrazzo generates striking patterns when you apply it to any part of an image. But Nance Paternoster has found that she gets the most beautiful patterns when she uses a source image that has many saturated colors, especially highly contrasting colors. When applied to this type of image, Terrazzo produces patterns that appear to be three-dimensional.

# Variations on a Theme: Filters on Filters

These images—created by Cotati, California, artist Mark Landman—are experiments in filtering. All are derived from the same original image, an already heavily modified portrait of writer Neil Gaiman for *Mondo 2000* and its fearless art director, Bart Nagel. The original was based on a rather poor black-and-white snapshot of Gaiman. Creating something worthwhile from this shot was made even more challenging by the subject's dark glasses and leather coat, and the lack of contrast in the few features that weren't obscured.

Rather than simply colorize a dull picture, Landman decided to do a nonrepresentational portrait using Paint Alchemy. Unlike most filters, which apply one effect and composite it based on your selection mask, Paint Alchemy goes much farther and uses information in the image such as color, saturation and brightness to control multiple aspects of a sophisticated brushing engine.

To give Paint Alchemy input to work with, Landman converted the grayscale scan to RGB and brightly colorized it, adding a blue gradient to the background. After making a smaller version of the image, he experimented until he got the look he wanted. This made the process go much faster, and gave him a good idea of what the final version would look like. Saving that effect as a preset in Paint Alchemy, he adjusted Brush sizes and density to compensate for the larger size, then ran the filter on the original, larger image.

Nearly the entire effect of the original image—"Sandfella"—resulted from that one pass in Paint Alchemy, but the swirly textures in the highlights came from Aldus Gallery Effects's Glass filter. The trick was using a grayscale PICT version of the image to control the effect. To do this, Landman first converted a copy of the image to Grayscale mode and saved it as a PICT file. Then in Gallery Effects's Glass filter dialog box, he clicked on Surface Controls and opened the newly created PICT file. That allowed him to use the grayscale file to control the amount of filtering applied to the original image: the brighter the values of the grayscale image, the stronger the effect.

"Sandfella"—the original filtered image.

All subsequent images came from manipulating this one image. The main tools used were filters and Kai's Power Tips. Kai Krause has developed unique image-processing tricks unlike anyone else, and freely posts related tips on America Online as well as in various magazines. Landman credits Kai's tips on using the Calculate commands, now the Calculations and Apply Image command in 3.0, with enabling him to achieve unusual effects that couldn't be done using Photoshop's compositing commands. However, because he was combining two or more composite images to create these effects, he used 3.0's Apply Image command in the Image menu rather than the Calculations command, which works only on channels. Particularly useful is Difference mode (now available as a mode to be applied between two layers in 3.0). This becomes very complex and wonderfully unpredictable in color.

Since Difference requires two source images, he duplicated the original. The trick is to then modify this second image before calculating the difference between the two. Because the two images weren't exactly alike, he'd get various interference patterns—some are quite beautiful, others quite ugly. To find the good ones he had to keep many different versions open at once, intuitively playing with them, compositing them through the Apply Image command and saving the results he liked.

"Abalone 2" was the result of using Photoshop's Gaussian Blur filter on the original, then duplicating and offsetting (using the Offset filter). After each new image was calculated, Levels were adjusted if necessary. Multiple versions, with varying offsets and blurs, as well as adjustments of Levels, Hue and Saturation, were used to achieve this unexpected effect.

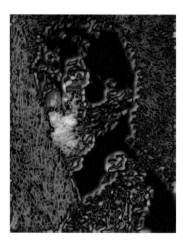

"Abalone 2."

"Purple Flamed" used higher levels of Gaussian blurring, and "inverted color" (a Hue wheel modification of 180, thanks Kai!). The shadows were then modified using the Gallery Effects's Glass filter and an inverted grayscale PICT.

"Purple Flamed."

"Jewelled Fog" used similar levels of blur, but midway through he used the Lighter command to achieve a lighter, airier feeling. The faint "oil slick" interference patterns were the result of applying the KPT Find Edges soft filter.

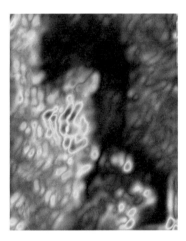

"Jewelled Fog."

"Plastik Man" used Motion Blur, followed by Gaussian Blur, to prepare the image for compositing with the Apply Image command. The wet, plastic look was created by Gallery Effects's Plastic Wrap filter. A slightly brighter and more luminous effect was achieved by applying the filter to a floating selection, then pasting using Luminance mode.

"Plastik Man."

"Hellish Impasto" also started with a Motion Blur filter application, this time at -45 degrees. Landman remixed it with the original file through the Apply Image command. Using this command with color images creates different effects than you'd get with simple compositing through a grayscale alpha channel. You can see patches of the original texture peeking through, as well as some color and texture from "Brown Fog."

"Hellish Impasto."

"Brown Fog" came out of the same "batch" as "Hellish Impasto," but was mixed more with other earlier variants, losing the Motion Blur, and breaking up into patches of different colors. Applying Gallery Effects's Glass filter using its default Frosted texture gave "Brown Fog" an even more complex look. This image also developed the solid, embossed sections of collar and eye/hair that would show up later in "Underwater."

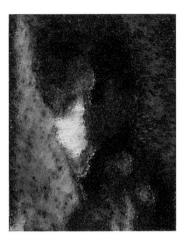

"Brown Fog."

"Poss. Jewel" was an outgrowth of "Brown Fog." You can see the brown structure that had developed on the left has morphed to a creamy pastel shade, and the complex spatters of the shadowed eye socket have been replaced by larger modulated blue patterns. These differences are the result of multiple composites using the Apply Image command as well as playing with Gallery Effects's Glass filter in different channels.

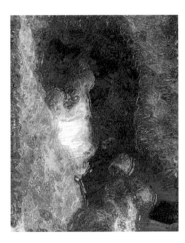

"Poss. Jewel."

"Glassy" skipped the blur filter applications and went straight to the Offset filter and Apply Image. This combination accentuated the original texture, giving rise to various embossed looks. A slight application of Gallery Effects's Texturizer filter, again using a grayscale version of the image, accentuated this look. Finally, color and contrast adjustments were made through the Hue and Levels commands.

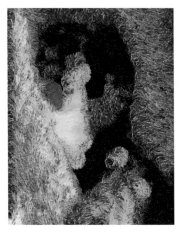

"Glassy."

"Sea Shell Colors" also omitted the blurring filters, but began with the "Brown Fog" and "Poss. Jewel" images, and used much smaller amounts of Offset filter to set up difference patterns. The result includes already-blurred areas that almost canceled each other out, leaving multicolored modulated grays, while complex, busy areas deposited flecks of bright varying hues.

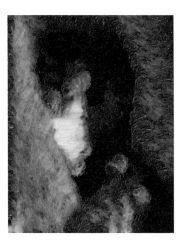

"Sea Shell Colors."

"Underwater" evolved from "Brown Fog." After making multiple copies of the original, Landman applied Motion Blur to each in different directions. As a result of running the images through varying, and sometimes random, calculations, he found the texture metamorphosed into areas of blurred bubbles, embossed striations, with "palette knife" textured borders. Another filter that had some effect is Gallery Effects's Plastic Wrap. You can see its characteristic sheen on the dark sections of jacket and eye/hair, though multiple use of Apply Image has removed the effect in other places.

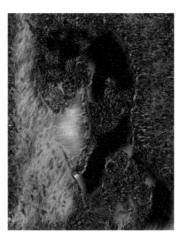

"Van Gone 2" combines "Brown Fog," "Poss. Jewel" and a version of "Underwater." You can see how GE's Plastic Wrap filter has created an inverted, raised section. As a final touch, he modified the image with the Hue/Saturation command. Although this image consists of the same ingredients as the other three, with no new tricks or filtering, the result is different.

"Van Gone 2."

## Making Terrazzo Patterns

Bay area artist and illustrator Diane Fenster has been playing with Xaos Tools's newest filter, Terrazzo, since she got her hands on the prerelease version. You can spend hours generating beautiful patterns with it, just as she has. Here are four examples.

## Tile 1

Fenster began with a stock photo from the Earth, Air, Fire & Water Collection. Using Terrazzo's Storm at Sea symmetry, she generated a tile. To use a tile as a pattern, open the tile, select All and copy.

The source image.

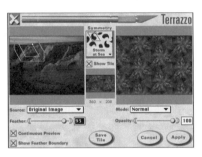

Terrazzo dialog box set up to generate the pattern.

The new tile.

After choosing Define Pattern (Edit menu), you must either open a new document or make a selection in a current file, choose Fill (Edit) and choose Pattern (Mode) in the Fill dialog box to get your final result. It's best to use this method rather than the Apply button because tiles are much smaller than patterns and therefore take up much less space. It's also imperative to use this technique if you want to preserve the original image you used to generate the tile; the Apply button applies the tile pattern to the entire original image.

The pattern generated from the tile.

## Tile 2

To create this tile, Fenster began with Tile 1 (described above). Selecting All, she manipulated it with Photoshop's Perspective command (Image>Effects) to change the angle of the tile and to put some white space around it. Using the same symmetry—Storm at Sea—as before, she made another tile, placing the selection border on the edge of the image to include a bit of the white background. This gave the new tile a ghostlike, feathery look and enhanced the perspective effect. Finally, she generated a pattern fill from the tile.

The distorted tile.

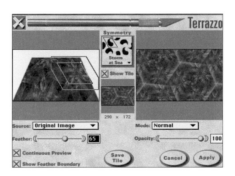

Selecting part of the tile from which to generate a new tile.

The new tile.

The pattern generated from the tile.

## Tile 3

For this tile, Fenster scanned in a sheet of rice paper to which she added squiggly brush strokes with Photoshop's brush tool. To generate the Terrazzo tile, she used the Pinwheel symmetry; then she generated the pattern.

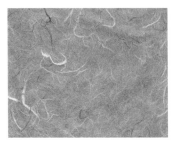

The original source image.

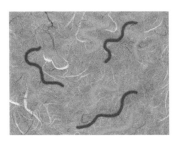

The image with brushstrokes applied.

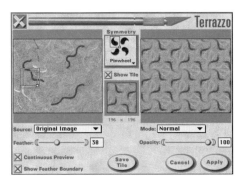

The Terrazzo settings that generated the pattern.

The pattern generated from the tile.

# Tile 4

After scanning a color calibration table, Fenster used Terrazzo's Whirlpool symmetry to generate this tile and pattern.

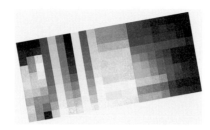

The source image—a color calibration table.

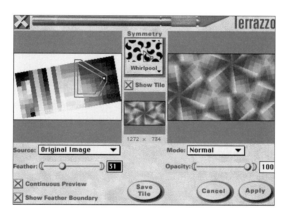

The Terrazzo dialog box with Whirlpool symmetry selected.

The Terrazzo tile.

The pattern generated from the tile.

**Artist:** Eve Elberg
**Image:** Swirls of Love
**Software:** Photoshop 3.0; Adobe Illustrator 5.5;
Kai's Power Tools 2.1; Paint Alchemy 1.0

Eve Elberg is an artist based in Brooklyn, New York, who frequently incorporates filters—native Photoshop and third-party—into her work. The effects in this image were generated by multiple applications of KPT's Fractal Explorer filter.

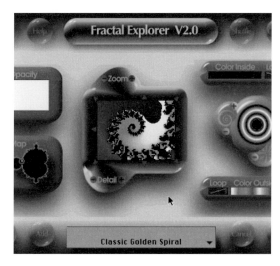

Choosing the preset Classic Golden Spiral from KPT Fractal Explorer.

By applying a variety of fractals and textures from Texture Explorer to various feathered selections, Elberg was able to build up an interesting look. She also used Paint Alchemy's Molecules Full style in heavily feathered selected areas. One of the resulting fractal curves she found particularly graceful-looking, so she decided to add some text to it.

Applying more preset textures from KPT Texture Explorer.

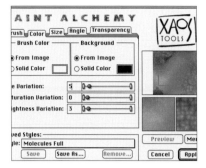

Applying the Molecules Full style from Paint Alchemy.

Creating a 72-dpi 1-bit version of the image, which she saved in PICT format, she opened it in Illustrator 5.5 as an underlying template. With the pen tool she traced a path along the predominant curve in the image. Then, with the text tool set to Text-on-a-Path mode, she clicked on the path she'd just drawn and used it as a baseline for the text. After kerning and positioning the type, she converted it to outlines and copied the selected outlines.

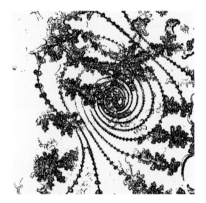

A 72-dpi 1-bit version of the image created for use as a template in Illustrator.

Tracing a path along the central curve.

Using the path as a
baseline for the text.

Back in Photoshop, Elberg created an alpha channel and pasted
the type as smooth, anti-aliased bitmaps. Using selections, feathering and additional filtering, she was able to add an element of
depth to the type to create a romantic, dreamlike image.

**Artist:** Eve Elberg
**Image**: Ancient Magic Board Game
**Software**: Photoshop 3.0; Terrazzo 1.0; Kai's Power Tools 2.1; PainterX2

Eve Elberg is another artist who can't resist Terrazzo. Fascinated by the image mutations generated by different tiling methods, she tried the filters on type, photos, line art and random blobs.

Curious about the visual aspect of the tools she was using, including Photoshop 3.0, Elberg began taking screen shots of assorted floating palettes, scroll bars and zoom boxes and applied Terrazzo to them. Deciding that the foreground and background color pickers would add interesting elements to a screen shot of the Photoshop toolbox, she isolated the bottom part of the toolbox and added extra white space using the Canvas Size command.

The bottom part of the Photoshop toolbox with white space added.

She began experimenting with different symmetries. After saving a few symmetries as tiles, she brought them into PainterX2 to see what would happen if she defined them as paper textures.

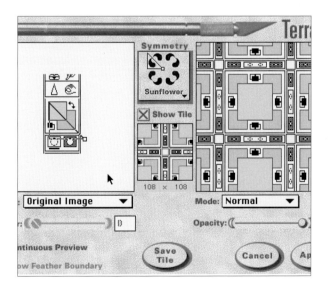

Experimenting with different symmetries in Terrazzo.

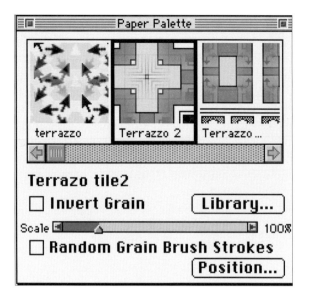

Symmetries
defined as
paper textures
in PainterX2.

After applying different paper textures, she saved the results for further editing in Photoshop. Back in Photoshop she touched them up a bit, did some image adjustment and used Terrazzo once more to define a seamlessly repeating tile.

The seamlessly repeating
Terrazzo tile.

She defined that tile as a pattern using Select All and then Edit/Define Pattern and filled a new document with it. In the Lighting Effects dialog box, she defined and applied a new spotlight with shiny and metallic attributes.

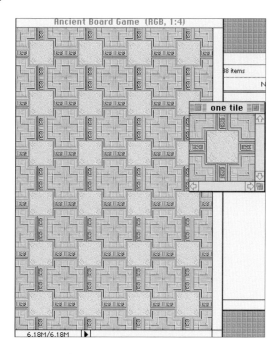

The tile defined as a pattern and used to fill a new file.

After adding half an inch all around the patterned rectangle using the Canvas Size command, she used the rectangular marquee to select the patterned area and feathered the selection by 45 pixels. Finally, she applied KPT's Gradients on a Path.

Applying KPT's Gradients on a Path to the pattern.

**Artist:** Ruth Kedar
**Image:** Diffusion
**Software:** Photoshop 3.0; Andromeda Series 1 Filters

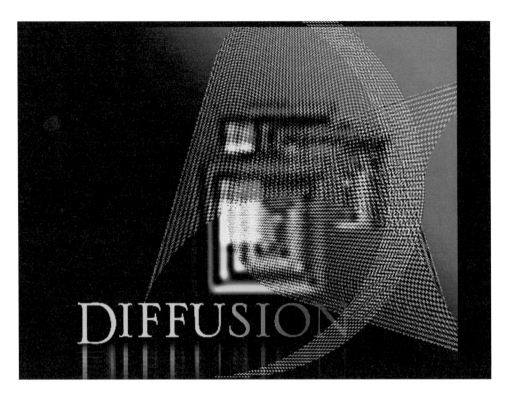

Ruth Kedar, an illustrator and artist who's thoroughly comfortable with filters, designed this image to illustrate a promotional brochure for Andromeda Series 1 Filters and to show some unusual—and unexpected—ways they can be used. For example, she used the Designs filter to create some interesting patterns and by reapplying them was able to create even more striking moiré patterns.

Beginning with a gradation in the background, Kedar used the brush tool to draw the concentric square element, which she duplicated twice and colorized.

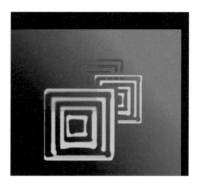

Original drawing.

She applied the Andromeda Series 1 Designs filter, which lets you create a dimensional shape on which you can map a variety of patterns. After choosing one of the Mezzo patterns, she bent it and squashed it to create a cylindrical effect.

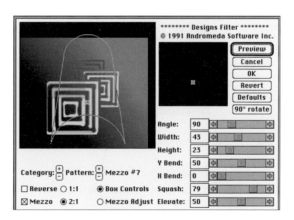

The settings for the first application of the Andromeda Designs filter.

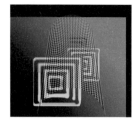

The result of the settings from the first application of the Andromeda Designs filter.

This also changed the original look of the pattern. Before reapplying the filter, she changed some of the settings: Angle, Width, Height, X Bend and Squash—to define the shape and position of the dimensional shape to which the pattern was applied, which again distorted the pattern itself.

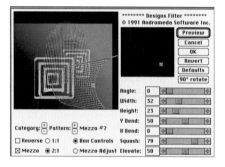

The settings for the second Designs filter application.

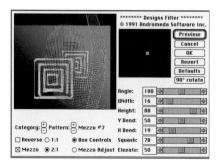

The image that resulted from the second Designs filter application.

For a third time she changed the settings to further refine the image.

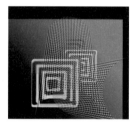

The settings for the third application.

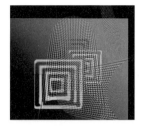

The result of the third application settings.

After adding a new layer, she enlarged the canvas size and used the type tool to type the word "Diffusion." Now she could modify the text—selecting the "D" and enlarging and repositioning it—without affecting the rest of the image. Additionally, she kerned the type using the rectangular marquee and the magic wand set at 254 pixels.

After checking the Preserve Transparency box on the Layers palette, she set the foreground color to yellow and the background to purple. Using the gradient tool, she made a linear blend from foreground to background, then merged the layers.

After the gradient fill was applied to the type and the layers were merged.

To give a high-gloss reflective effect to the area around the type, Kedar used the Andromeda Velocity filter instead of the Reflection filter because she wanted a sharper and more controlled blend. In the Velocity dialog box, she selected Local Area Blur, set the angle at 90 degrees, # of Copies to 13 and Spacing to 10.

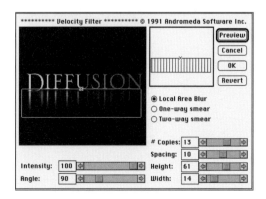

The Andromeda Velocity filter settings.

**Artist:** Ruth Kedar
**Image:** Gridlock & the Time Bubble
**Software:** Photoshop 3.0; Andromeda Series 2 3D Filter

This image was done to illustrate a promotional brochure for the Andromeda Series 2 3D filter, to show off its versatility. Using only a scanned image of a chronometer, Kedar created a collage that seems to be many different elements. That, however, is strictly an illusion; there are actually just two elements, each treated with the 3D filter in various ways that result in radically different effects.

After opening the scan of the chronometer, Kedar created a new layer, filled it with white and applied the Andromeda 3D filter to create a grid on a plane surface.

Original scan of chronometer.

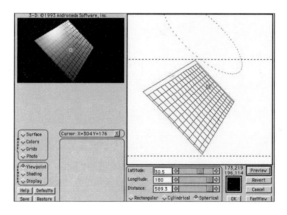

Andromeda dialog box with Plane surface selected.

The result of the 3D filter applied to the layer.

On the Layers palette, she composited the chronometer with the grid, setting mode to Multiply and opacity to 70 percent. Then, selecting the Background layer, she duplicated it and named it "Bubble." With the elliptical marquee, she selected the chronometer face and applied the 3D filter with the Spherical setting to give it a bubblelike effect.

Compositing the chronometer and the grid.

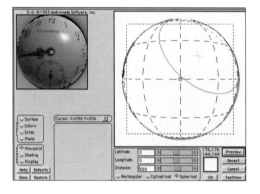

Andromeda 3D filter dialog box with Sphere surface selected.

For a drop shadow effect, Kedar added a layer mask to the Bubble layer, creating a feathered selection slightly larger than the bubble, filled it with black and offset it slightly from the bubble. Double-clicking on the layer mask to bring up the layer mask options, she clicked on the Color Indicates Visible Areas radial button to make the background layer show through.

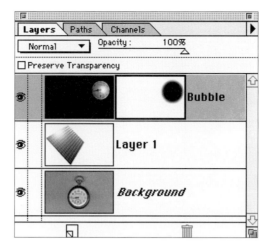

The Photoshop 3.0 Layers palette showing the chronometer, the grid and the spherized chronometer face and its associated layer mask.

After flattening the layers, she saved the image as "Collage" and enlarged the canvas size to fill it with a black background.

After the layer elements were composited and the layers were flattened.

Next she opened the original chronometer scan and duplicated the background layer. Using the 3D filter again, she created a new view of the chronometer, which she called "Plane 1 Layer."

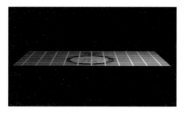

The chronometer wrapped onto the plane with grid visible (saved as "Plane 1").

She selected Plane 1 with the pen tool, saved that selection as a layer mask for Plane 1 and hid the layer. Selecting the background layer again, she applied the 3D filter to create another three-dimensional view of the chronometer.

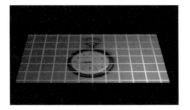

The chronometer wrapped onto the plane with the same settings except Viewpoint latitude set to a different perspective (saved as "Plane 2").

Now she had a Background layer and the Plane 1 layer with a layer mask. Finally, she merged the layers before pasting them into the final image. [f/x]

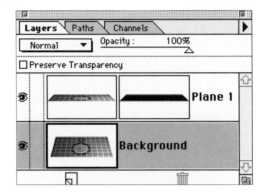

The layers ready to be merged.

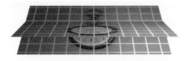

Planes 1 and 2 ready to be pasted into the final image.

# CHAPTER 3

# Photoshop f/x:
# Using Other Programs
# With Photoshop

Many images in this book were created entirely in Photoshop. But just as many were done with Photoshop in conjunction with other applications. Other Adobe products like Illustrator and Dimensions are obvious examples of programs whose strengths fill in some weaknesses and nicely complement Photoshop's capabilities.

## Adobe Illustrator

Because it's a PostScript-based object-oriented draw program, Illustrator is perfect for generating and positioning type that's needed in a Photoshop image. For example, if you've created an object in Photoshop that will have text wrapped around it, you can create a path in Photoshop and export it to Illustrator. There you can type your text along a path, convert the text to outlines, then save the file and place it into a channel in your Photoshop document. You simply load the selection in Photoshop and then either fill your type, use Levels or Curves to darken the text with the background, paste another image into it or perform any other manipulation that sounds appealing. Of course, it's always preferable to place your Photoshop document in Illustrator and not rasterize the type, because when you rasterize type you fix its resolution, whereas if you are able to leave the type in a PostScript it will always print at the maximum resolution. That's not possible if you want to load it as a selection and adjust Curves or apply some other effect that can only be done in an image-processing program like Photoshop.

## Dimensions & Add Depth

Simple 3D shape generators like Dimensions and Ray Dream's Add Depth are great for quickly and easily building simple three-dimensional objects like the bottle artist Ruth Kedar made for use in her Desert Wind series of fine art images. They're certainly a lot easier to use than are the full-strength and much less intuitive 3D modeling programs.

## Fractal Design Painter

Several artists featured in this book frequently go back and forth between Photoshop and Painter. They love to incorporate Painter's wonderfully diverse brushes and textures into their work, but always return to Photoshop for additional manipulations, its compositing capabilities and its CMYK support. Although not specifically designed to work well together (as Illustrator, Dimensions and Photoshop were), Painter and Photoshop are excellent complements to each other, as much of the artwork in this book proves.

> **TIP: USING CLIPPING PATHS IN PHOTOSHOP**
>
> If you want to use a clipping path in Photoshop but are concerned about trapping it in your page layout program try this tip from Julieanne Kost. Export your clipping path to Illustrator. Highlight the path and make a duplicate of it. Move the duplicate to another layer on top of the first. Stroke the path and set it to overprint. Then hide that layer. Import the Photoshop file without the path and mask it with the path in Illustrator. Then make the layer with the stroked path visable. Save the file as an EPS and place that into your page layout program. This works only if the color around the path in Photoshop is a solid color, since the stroke can only be one color.

## 3D Modeling Programs

Only a relatively small percentage of artists thrive in the world of true 3D modeling; these programs are not known for ease of use or intuitive interfaces. Most artists stick to two-dimensional imagery or maybe just sporadically dabble in 3D art. But many of these modelers are easier than they used to be, and if you're willing to endure the learning curve, you can possibly produce some striking three-dimensional objects to place into your Photoshop creations. One artist who has skillfully combined 3D imagery with Photoshop images is Greg Vander Houwen. He has discovered some wonderful techniques, evident in the work displayed later in this chapter.

# Live Picture

This program is a boon for artists who must work with massive files, since its proprietary FITS technology mathematically represents images. Unlike Photoshop's, Live Picture's layers don't add huge amounts of data to your files, and the program can perform various manipulations, such as rotating and scaling, much more quickly than Photoshop can. However, it lacks the depth and breadth of Photoshop's many image-editing functions. The artists I know who use Live Picture consider it a good program but not a substitute for Photoshop. John Lund's *New Wave Research,* featured in this chapter, is an example of using Live Picture in conjunction with Photoshop. Its weaknesses are Photoshop's strengths, and therefore, the two are often used on the same image.

# Specular Collage

Just because Photoshop 3.0's Layers feature now lets you composite numerous floating selections at the same time doesn't mean that Collage is obsolete. Collage's advantage is that it lets you work very quickly and render the final image after the fact. Because Collage creates low-res proxies of your images, you can quickly and easily composite elements, put them in the foreground or background, or duplicate images to have one part in the background and the other in the foreground. In Collage, the design process is much faster and requires less storage space because it doesn't generate massive image files. Jeff Brice, an enthusiastic Collage user whose images appear in this chapter and in the Gallery, sees no reason to throw it away, just because Photoshop now has layers. Without Collage, Brice would have found it much more time-consuming to conceptualize an image like *Windmachine* (see page 84).

As with Chapter 2, "Third-Party Filters," this chapter is not intended to be an exhaustive study of all the programs that work well with Photoshop or all the ways these programs complement each other. It's designed just to get you started in a good direction. Where you go from there is entirely up to you.

# Case Studies

Below are some examples of images created with Photoshop in conjunction with some of the programs I've mentioned. Of course, there are many more examples to be found out there. But these examples of the ways Photoshop can be—and is—used with other programs should give you some intriguing ideas of what you can do with  similar combinations of tools.

**Artist:** Jeff Brice
**Image:** Windmachine
**Software:** Photoshop; Specular Collage 1.0.1; Kai's Power Tools 2.0

Brice composited 17 scanned photos—all taken by the artist himself—to produce this collage for his fine art portfolio. In Photoshop
he enhanced the colors and created a mask for each image. But
instead of creating distinct masks that closely defined selected
objects in the photos, he made soft, blurry masks for sections of
each photo. Then—because the masks were not well defined and
didn't correspond to the shapes of any
of the objects—when he layered the elements in Collage, they appeared to
overlap and blend into each other, without any clear boundaries between them.
This resulted in a rich textural background in which no single element
stood out. Brice also used KPT's
Gradient Designer to add the multicolor
gradation in the clouds. In Photoshop
3.0 he could have achieved the same
effect by putting each image on a different layer with a layer mask instead of
bringing them into Collage, but Brice
prefers to experiment with compositing
images in Collage because he can work
much more quickly on low-res proxies
than on full-blown image files.

> **TIP: SIMULATING GRADATIONS IN COLLAGE**
> Since you can't create gradations
> in Collage, Brice uses a solid
> white box with a horizontal white-
> to-black gradation and one with a
> diagonal gradation to place
> behind an element that needs to
> be brightened. The gradated box
> shows through to punch up the
> overlying image. To create a
> ghosting effect, place the box over
> the element. You can use this
> technique to brighten up or ghost
> part of the image as well as cre-
> ate a shadow by inverting the
> box's RGB channel.

**Artist:** Stuart Bradford
**Image:** Right Balance
**Software:** Photoshop 3.0; Illustrator 5.5

Bradford finds that Illustrator works well with Photoshop for positioning and sizing elements by creating templates and channels. You can create complex masks with Illustrator's more powerful and easy-to-use tools that you can then import into Photoshop.

For this image (done for *Selling Networks*, a supplement of *LAN Times* magazine), Bradford began by compiling digital stock photos from which he would later composite elements to place inside the arc shape. Next he scanned in a rough pencil sketch and placed it in Illustrator. There he used it to create a template for roughing out the shapes and their positions in the illustration.

**TIP: USING ILLUSTRATOR FOR SPOT COLORS**
You can posterize photographs and take them through Adobe Streamline into Illustrator, where you can add spot colors. This process is especially popular with silkscreen printers.

The rough pencil sketch scanned and opened in Illustrator.

The template that was used for positioning the elements.

After copying the line-art template in Illustrator, he pasted it into a channel (Template channel) in Photoshop to use as a template he could refer to while working in RGB mode to get accurate positioning as he imported the individual masks (of the large and small arcs and the steps) from Illustrator. To work on the arc-shaped area, he marqueed just the arc part of the template, and saved it to a new channel (Arc template). With the template visible beneath the RGB channel, he began arranging and compositing the various photo fragments, still using the template as a guide.

The template of just the arc shape.

Back in Illustrator, he copied the arc shape and pasted it into another channel in Photoshop to use as a mask. After correctly positioning the mask to match up with the template, he inverted it to make the mask white and the background black (when brought in from Illustrator, it's always the reverse) and went back to the RGB channel and loaded the mask. He then copied the arc-shaped image and pasted it into the main illustration. To correctly position it in the main illustration, he turned on the template channel and lined up the arc-shaped image with the template, then used the same process with the smaller shape and image inside the arc. With the other elements, he also used the template for accurate positioning and resizing.

The arc mask.

The arc template showing through the RGB channel.

To add the type, he saved the illustration as an EPS file and placed it in Illustrator. Then using the line tool, he drew some paths and typed words on the path. Once he'd edited and positioned the type, he selected and copied it and pasted it into a channel of the illustration in Photoshop and with all the channels visible but only the type channel writable, he moved the type into position. Bradford then loaded the channel and filled it with color.

> **TIP: MASKS IN ILLUSTRATOR**
> Creating masks in Illustrator (using objects like type or shapes) lets you import Photoshop textures and photographs into Illustrator while still preserving Illustrator's PostScript outlines. Illustrator is also great for creating masks and loading them into Photoshop as selections.

**Artist:** Jeff Brice
**Image:** Fountain
**Software**: Photoshop 3.0; Specular Collage 1.0.1;
Kai's Power Tools 2.0

Bradford then loaded the channel and filled it with color.

For this fine art piece, Brice first scanned in the photos of the fountain and the constellation chart. The fountain image was actually a combination of seven different photos Brice physically composited before scanning, which explains its unusual shape.

The original composite of seven different photos of the fountain.

After creating an alpha channel, he made the red channel visible and the alpha channel both visible and editable (by clicking on the channel). He selected the fountain in the alpha channel, where he created a black-to-white gradation (from black at the top to white at the bottom). Positioning the gradation at the bottom half of the fountain, he left the top half completely black (without any gradation).

The gradation in the alpha channel (here tinted red) with the red channel (shown here in grayscale) also visible.

Brice went back to the RGB channel and loaded the selection of the gradation, then created a floating selection. Opening KPT's Gradient Designer, he selected Gentle Gold in the Metallic submenu and used the angle tool to apply it at a 45° angle. This applied a light-to-dark gold gradation over the fountain that shows through the mask to affect only the bottom half of the fountain. Using a floating selection allowed him to use Layer Options, which gave him much more control over the image.

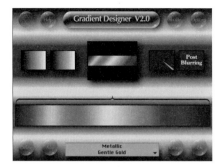

KPT's Gradient Designer filter dialog box with Gentle Gold color gradient selected.

KPT's Gradient Designer filter applied to the floating selection.

In Layer Options, he set the opacity to 65 percent and the mode to Color, which changed the colors while maintaining their values (lightness and darkness). Then he defloated the image (Command-j). Next he "Selected All" in the alpha channel and flipped the alpha channel (Image>Flip>Vertical) to apply the same gradation in the top half but in the opposite direction (white-to-black). Back in the RGB channel, Brice loaded the selection, which allowed him to change the colors through the gradation, using the gradation to determine how the colors would be affected (the lighter the area, the more it would change).

The flipped alpha channel, which reversed the gradient's direction for use in the upper section of the image.

In the Curves dialog box, he changed the colors by shifting the curve in the Blue channel.

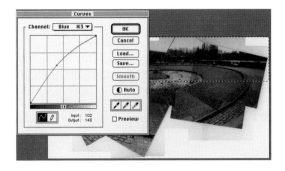

Manipulating Curves to shift the colors from gray to blue.

Brice created a mask in Photoshop that would be used for compositing all the images once they'd been imported into Collage. Using the same alpha channel he'd used for the other masks, and with the red channel visible and the alpha channel visible and editable, he selected everything in the alpha channel and filled it with black. Then he outlined the fountain with the lasso while holding down the option key (to draw a straight line). To gradate a small area of the mask, he used the gradation tool to drag from the top of the fountain down about half an inch; this ended the gradation at that point and filled the rest of the selection with white. Once the elements were placed in Collage, only the white areas were affected, while the black areas dropped out.

The final mask that was used for compositing the fountain in Collage.

The fountain ready to be composited in Collage.

**Artist:** Nance Paternoster
**Image:** OcchiAzzuri
**Software:** Photoshop 3.0; Painter 2.0; PainterX2

Nance Paternoster is a San Francisco artist who works with 2D, 3D and animated imagery. The artist began by scanning a black-and-white photo of a friend into Photoshop. The background image was begun in Fractal Design Painter, where she used the airbrush and chalk to lay down the basic colors. After importing the background image into Photoshop, she created a channel for the border area that frames the image and pasted some scanned textures into the channel. To add more depth to the background, she loaded the selection and used the airbrush to lighten and darken areas around the textures. After selecting the border and darkening it, she again used the airbrush to lighten and darken areas around the textures.

The original photo of the figure.

The image after textures were added in Painter.

Next Paternoster created a mask for the wings into which she would paste some of the angel images she had previously scanned. First she cleaned up the scans by deleting the background areas around the angels. With the magic wand set to a tolerance of 1, she selected each angel individually and then applied a 3-pixel feather radius. After pasting the angels into the wings mask, she used Layer Options in Normal mode with 60 percent opacity.

Close-up of
original wings.

Close-up of wings with
three angels pasted
into them.

For one of the angels, she used a different technique. Because
pasting into the wings mask would have cut off the tops of the
angel's wings and the bottom of her dress, she opted to use the
Paste command rather than the Paste Into command so that she
could float the angel over the wing without having the selection
border of the wing cut off the pasted angel. To make the angel
transparent, she then used Layer Options in Normal mode with
50 percent opacity.

Still in Photoshop, Paternoster applied the dodge/burn/sponge
tool to add highlights and shadows to the figure. Back in Painter,
she also used the Fat Stroke variant of the airbrush with Soft Paint
Remover and Soft Paint Thickener methods to give the wings more
dimension. In Photoshop, Paternoster duplicated the angel in the
top-left corner. Then after darkening the original with the Brightness/
Contrast command, she pasted the lighter duplicate over the original and then applied the airbrush and the dodge and burn options
of the dodge/burn/sponge tool to simulate shadows. In Painter she

created a fiery texture in the top-right corner—with the Smeary Mover variant of Painter's Liquid Brush—to match the angel she would later paste into it.

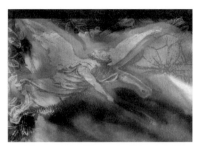

Detail of angel in top-left corner.

Next, she tinted the body by adjusting the hue in Photoshop. After importing this version into Painter, she cloned it and made a frisket of the body, then cleared the selected area. Using the Chalk Cloner variant of the Cloner brush, she repainted the entire figure with a chalk texture. Back in Photoshop, she copied and pasted his hair and face separately onto the repainted body, so she could tint the hair (by changing the hue) without altering the face (she didn't want it to have the painted texture of the body). With Photoshop's airbrush, she added a little texture and depth; she also used the dodge and burn tools in both Painter and Photoshop (since they act differently: Painter provides more options and larger brushes) to lighten and darken different parts of the figure.

Figure cloned with Painter's Chalk Cloner brush and pasted onto original.

Once again in Photoshop, Paternoster pasted various images into or behind different areas of the background—which she'd previously saved as selection masks—using Layer Options in different modes, such as Luminosity, Multiply and Lighten. Zeroing in on the lower-right corner reveals many layers of textures and selections scaled to different perspectives and pasted into the selection. In Photoshop, she used the airbrush once again to lighten and darken certain areas and to give the body and face a three-dimensional look. Finally, the eyes were selected and tinted with the Variations command.

**Artist:** Greg Vander Houwen
**Image:** Reflections on Subtle Matter
**Software:** Photoshop 2.5.1, 3.0; StrataVision 3D 2.0

Vander Houwen frequently mixes Photoshop and 3D imagery to achieve striking results. He originally created this image using Photoshop 2.5, but recently updated it in 3.0. It illustrates a great technique that uses Photoshop to simplify the modeling of a three-dimensional object.

Vander Houwen composited the image from four primary elements: photos of a forest and a sunset, a three-dimensional model of a room and a woman's figure created in Photoshop.

The birch forest came from a photograph he took outside Flagstaff, Arizona. The room was rendered entirely in StrataVision 3D; its surface maps and much of its geometry—for example, the stained-glass door—were extracted from images Vander Houwen created in Photoshop.

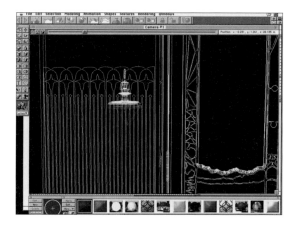

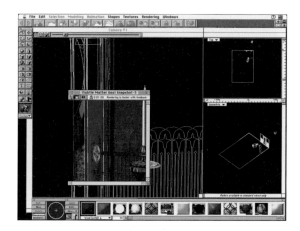

Two different views of the room being modeled in StrataVision 3D.

After drawing the lead design for the door in Illustrator, he rasterized it in Photoshop. Converting the image to a bitmap (which meant it had no gray levels) and saving it in PICT format made it possible for StrataVision to extract the geometry of the stained-glass leading.

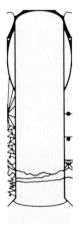

The original stained-glass lead design drawn in Illustrator.

He created the bump map, which gave the lead its 3D look, by applying the Emboss filter on the original rasterized lead image. He created the glass geometry in much the same way, except that in Photoshop he inverted the map of the original image so that Strata would extract the inverse geometry. Vander Houwen considers this technique a major discovery, since it allows him to transform very complex line art into skeletel geometry.

The original door, the bump map of the door created by the Emboss filter and the door with its map inverted.

The woman reflected in the glass was painted in Photoshop and then mapped to an object behind camera view in the Strata model. The sunset, which came from a photograph taken in the foothills of the Cascades, was mapped to an object behind the door in the Strata model. The rendered room and the forest were then composited into the main image.

To make the forest appear to be behind the wall, Vander Houwen pasted it on top of the rendered 3D room at a low opacity. Then using the lasso tool—set to a light feather—he held down the command key and traced around the candles and the door. This deleted the candles and the door area from the floating selection. After saving the selection, he loaded the selection again and used the Paste Into command (Edit menu) to paste the candle and door selection into the forest image as he'd done before, but this time at 100 percent opacity. Then after setting a large feather in the Lasso dialog box, he command-selected away soft chunks of the forest image until he got the look he wanted. Finally, to make the foreground blend more with the background, he painted shadows and highlights on the tree roots and the rocks in the forest image.

## TIP: AUTOMATING COMPLEX SELECTIONS

You can use images to mask themselves—as Greg Vander Houwen does—to create complex selections. To extract a selection from a color image, first find and activate the channel with the most contrast in the areas you want to select, then copy its contents to a new channel. Using Levels or Curves, boost the contrast in the new channel to isolate the desired selection areas. Finally, go back to the composite RGB channel and load the manipulated channel as a selection.

**Artist:** John Lund
**Image:** New Wave Research
**Software:** Photoshop 3.0; Live Picture 1.0

John Lund is a heavy user of both Photoshop and Live Picture. He often goes from one to the other in the course of completing a photo-illustration such as this one.

Lund scanned two 35mm color slides—a background image and a scientist at work in his laboratory—and opened them in Photoshop. There he selected all the background and applied the Radial Blur filter, setting Amount to 100, Blur Method to Zoom and Quality to Good. Again he selected the entire background and in the Hue/Saturation window, boosted the saturation to 50 percent and saved it as a TIFF file.

The original background image.

The background after it was distorted in Photoshop.

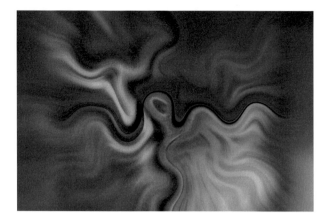

The background after it was distorted in Live Picture.

From there he brought the background image into Live Picture, converting it to Live Picture's proprietary IVUE format. Then he opened a new file in Live Picture and inserted the background (Create>Image Distort) at 100 percent in Auto Insert mode. In Creative mode, he chose Distort under the Paintbrush option and clicked the third-largest brush. Using the Wacom tablet, he distorted the image as he drew and painted over it, then saved it in Live Picture's FITS format.

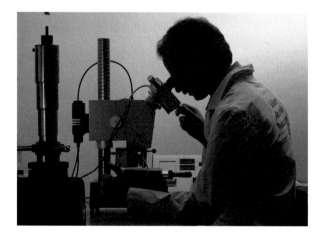

The photo of the scientist.

Next he inserted the photo of the scientist (Create>Image Insertion) at 100 percent with Auto Insert off. In Creative mode, he clicked on the Eraser, chose a large brush and erased selected areas of the image. To paint back some of the erased areas, he selected the Paintbrush, then chose an opacity and the appropriate brush size. After saving in FITS format, he built the final file, adding 3 percent noise.

## Creating simple 3D imagery for Photoshop

For the fine art piece, *Desert Wind 2*, described in the Step-by-Step Gallery on page 192, Kedar used Adobe Dimensions to create the simple, curved bottle that she incorporated into her Photoshop image and in fact all the images in her Desert Wind series. She wanted to evoke a mystical, enchanted, fable-like world of mirages and buried treasure. To provide a sense of that surreal world, she combined existing elements such as photographs and objects with drawn elements like the bottle. Using Dimensions allowed her to quickly and easily create a graceful-looking bottle that she imported into her Photoshop image for further manipulation.

She began by creating a profile for the bottle in Illustrator, which she imported into Dimensions. There she used the Revolve command to create the bottle's three-dimensional shape.

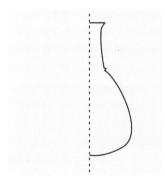

Bottle profile drawn in Dimensions.

Revolved bottle in Dimensions.

Back in Illustrator, Kedar created a design for mapping onto the bottle's surface. In Dimensions 2.0's Mapped Artwork window, she positioned the design on the bottle, then rendered the image. From there, she simply placed the 3D bottle in Photoshop and incorporated it into her existing image.

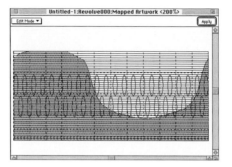

Surface design drawn in Dimensions's Mapped Artwork window (light area represents visible surface of bottle).

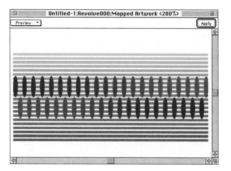

Surface design previewed in color (Dimensions's Preview mode).

With the surface design wrapped around it, the bottle was ready to be imported into the Photoshop image.

## Rendering Background Alpha Channels

To demonstrate this technique, Greg Vander Houwen extracted the candle geometry and maps from the model he used to create *Reflections on Subtle Matter* (see page 100). Placing the candle on a 3D plane, he mapped onto it a stock Strata black-and-white tile. He lit the environment with a dim neutral, ambient light source. In the immediate area of the candle, right at the flame, he placed a very small, warm light source object.

The wireframe of the candle.

Positioning the light source directly at the flame.

He raytraced the model in Strata StudioPro with the Render Background Alpha Channel box checked. This made Studio Pro render an RGB image as well as the selection mask needed to separate it from its background.

After the candle model
was raytraced in
StrataVision Studio Pro.

The candle's selection mask.

When he loaded the image into Photoshop, a quick look at the
Channels palette confirmed that the mask was there in the alpha
channel, so he just loaded the selection. He then inverted it to
enclose the black background and pasted some distant mountains
into the selection to complete the image. f/x

After the candle—along
with its mask—were
brought into Photoshop
and the mountains were
pasted into the
background.

# Section 2
## Step-by-Step Gallery

Working on Forms So That Forms Can Be

Jeff Brice

**Artist:** Jeff Brice
**Image:** Studio 1
**Software:** Photoshop 3.0; Specular Collage 1.0.1;
Kai's Power Tools 2.0

Jeff Brice

A Seattle-based illustrator who specializes in photo collages, Brice created this piece for his fine art portfolio. He began by painting a brushstroke in black ink, which he scanned in Grayscale mode and opened in Photoshop. After saving the grayscale brushstroke in an alpha channel, he used KPT Gradient Designer to create a radial gradient in the RGB channel and saved the image.

The tree branches were part of a photo Brice had taken himself, which he scanned in grayscale. To give the branches a pale purple tint—a simulated duotone effect—he colorized them in the Curves dialog box (Image> Adjust>Curves).

The original scan of the tree branches photo.

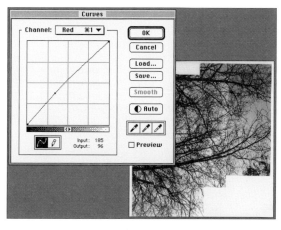

Color Curves applied to the tree branch scan in Photoshop.

To fade the branches at the upper right, he drew a small rectangle over the area and saved that as a selection, which automatically created a new alpha channel. Within the rectangle he created a diagonal gradation from black to white (in the alpha channel), and then filled the selection with white in the RGB channel to create a ghosting effect. Next he duplicated the tree branches; then flipped the copy to create a mirror image.

The gradated mask that was applied to an outer section of the branches.

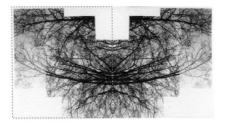

The tree branch image flipped in Photoshop.

Brice used a similar process to create a gradation over the center area of the branches. After drawing a rectangle over that area, he created a vertical gradation from white to black in an alpha channel; then he loaded the selection (the section of the branches encompassed by the rectangle) and inverted (Image>Map>Invert) it, using the gradation to determine the color values.

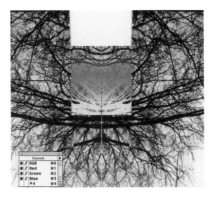

A second gradated mask (for the center section of the tree) after Brice inverted it.

The large, irregularly shaped multicolored brushstroke was painted on paper in black and scanned in grayscale.

The black brushstroke
scanned in grayscale.

In Photoshop he saved it to an alpha channel; then in the
RGB channel, he selected all. In KPT Gradient Designer, he
created a spectrum radial gradation and saved the RGB and the
alpha channels.

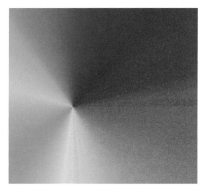

The radial gradation in
the RGB channel Brice
created with KPT
Gradient Designer that
would later be pushed
through the brushstroke
mask in Collage.

Previewing the RGB
channel (containing the
gradient) through the
brushstroke mask in the
alpha channel.

After scanning and making a mask for each of the other elements,
he imported them all into Collage and saved them.

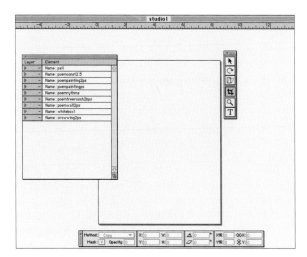

The first to be put onto Collage's working canvas were the two main elements: the tree and the wall (which was a photo of a wall in the artist's studio): these were sized down and positioned. Next to be added was the painted texture (hand-painted on a board with watercolors); Brice changed its layer to place it behind the wall.

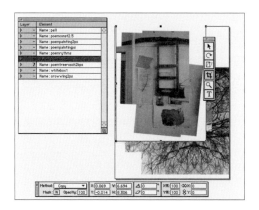

Compositing the wall and the tree branches in Collage.

To drop out the lighter areas of the wall and allow the paint texture to show through those areas, he applied Darken mode to the wall (Information window>Method>Darken). He darkened the tree by multiplying its color values in Multiply mode.

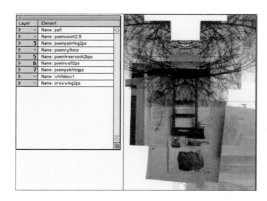

| Layer | Element |
|---|---|
| ▶ | Name: pafl |
| ▶ | Name: poemconst2.5 |
| ▶ 3 | Name: poempainting2ps |
| ▶ | Name: poemrhythms |
| ▶ 5 | Name: poemtreerosch2bps |
| ▶ 6 | Name: poemwall2ps |
| ▶ 7 | Name: poempaintingps |
| ▶ | Name: whitebox1 |
| ▶ | Name: crowwing2ps |

Adding the paint texture layer to the composite.

The multicolored brushstroke was added to the canvas and its mask was turned on to make the colors in the radial gradation show through the grayscale mask. The line chart was then placed over the brushstroke.

After putting the constellation at the top edge of the tree branches, Brice cropped it and duplicated it, then moved the copy to the lower left of the illustration underneath the brushstroke.

Because the wall was on top of the paint texture and in Darken mode, the white streak took on the gray value of the wall, and therefore didn't show as prominently as Brice wanted it to. To make the white streak more visible, he duplicated the texture, cropped out everything but the white streak and composited it in Lighten mode.

The center part of the wall was hidden by the branches. To make it visible, he duplicated the wall, cropped it and composited it onto the top layer. f/x

**Artist:** Diane Fenster
**Image:** La Belle Helene
**Software:** Photoshop 2.5.1; Specular Collage
1.0.1; Terrazzo; FotoMagic; Fractal Design Painter

Diane Fenster is an illustrator and fine artist based in the San Francisco Bay area. She created this image for *Macworld* magazine to illustrate a review of Specular Collage. Fenster began by selecting an image from a photo CD collection, a fireworks display as a base image from which to create a background texture.

The original fireworks image.

After opening it in Photoshop, she applied Xaos Tools's Terrazzo filter, which automatically generates unusual shapes and patterns from any section of an image. Once she found a pattern she liked, she altered it by applying Photoshop's Ripple filter, which gave it a wavy texture.

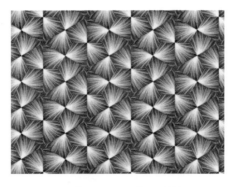

The first pattern created with Terrazzo.

The Ripple filter applied to the Terrazzo pattern.

Next, Fenster changed the pattern's colors from gold, orange and brown to blue-green, beige and rust shades, using the Color Balance and Hue/Saturation commands. To give it more texture, she imported it into Fractal Design Painter, where she applied the Acid Etch surface texture from Painter's Paper Texture library. From there she brought it back into Photoshop, where she used the lasso with a 25-pixel-radius feather to make a selection. To select everything but the lassoed area and delete it, she used the Inverse command under the Select menu. Next she made a copy of the Terrazzo pattern without the Painter texture applied and pasted that into the background area surrounding the feathered selection. Using the Scale command (Image>Effects), she enlarged it until it completely filled the background area. Again using Color Balance and Hue/Saturation, she darkened the colors to brick red and blue-green.

The pattern after its colors were changed and it was imported into Fractal Design Painter, where the Acid Etch texture was applied.

The pattern after the feathered selection was made and the area around it was deleted.

The face was actually a white porcelain pin that Fenster scanned. Using Ring of Fire's FotoMagic ColorRanger II filter, she applied its Sepia setting to the face. Then she applied the Transparent Gold setting of the same filter to the sepia-tone image.

The original scan of the porcelain pin.

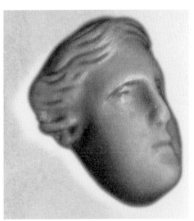

The pin after the sepia setting of the FotoMagic ColorRanger II filter was applied.

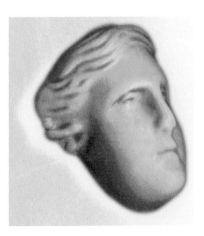

The pin after the Transparent Gold setting of the ColorRanger II filter was used.

The bicycle and rider were scanned from a piece of clip art. In Photoshop, Fenster applied the Solarize filter, adjusted the Levels to brighten the colors and increased the Hue to +126.

The original scan of the bicycle and rider.

After the bicycle and rider were solarized and color levels were adjusted.

The bicycle and rider after the Hue was adjusted to +126.

Using the path tool, she made a mask for each of these elements before importing them into Collage. For the mask of the face, she used a feather of 9 pixels to create a soft edge around it.

After importing all the elements into Collage for layering, she duplicated the bicycle and rider twice, making each one successively smaller and manipulating each one differently. On the first duplicate, she used the Method command with the Multiply option and opacity of 90 percent. On the second duplicate, she used the Subtract Method with 60 percent opacity. *Note:* This image was originally created in Photoshop 2.5.1 and what was done in Collage can now be done in Photoshop 3.0 using layers in Multiply and Subtract modes and layer masks. However, the benefits of using Collage are still valid: you can work more quickly with low-res versions of images, switching back to high-res when you've finalized your layout. f/x

**Artist:** Annabelle Breakey
**Image:** Carousel
**Software:** Photoshop 3.0

Annabelle Breakey is a San Francisco-based photographer and photo-illustrator. This image evolved from a black-and-white photo Breakey took of the antique carousel at San Francisco's Golden Gate Park, which she scanned into Photoshop.

Original scan of
the carousel.

Breakey loved the look of the delicately carved horses but not the mundane background surrounding them. So to build a new background for the image, she found a scan of some blades of grass that had been previously cut out of another photo and manipulated: the background area around the grass had been dropped out and some blades duplicated.

Scan of the
grass photo.

After drawing a path around the horses with the pen tool,
Breakey made a selection of the area with a 30-pixel feather to create a soft, semitransparent edge around the horses. She then used
the Inverse command to select the background area so she could
paste the grass into it. Because the carousel image was grayscale,
the grass became grayscale as well once it became part of the image.
Through the feather edge around the background areas, the grass
and the horses blended into each other. Next she flipped the grass,
so that it would appear to be moving in the same direction as the
horses. To fill the entire area around the horses—and to make the
grass lush, thick and junglelike—she copied the original grass
image and pasted it numerous times until it completely obliterated
the original background behind the carousel.

Detail of grass
after it was
repasted
numerous times.

After making a duplicate of the entire image, Breakey applied Photoshop's Gaussian Blur filter with a 30-pixel radius to it and copied and pasted that into the selection of the horses.

Gaussian Blur filter applied to a duplicate of the carousel image.

After pasting a duplicate of the image onto another layer and blurring the duplicate layer, Breakey used Layer Options to change opacity to 80 percent and mode to Lighten. This produced glowing, diffused highlights, giving the horses an ethereal, dreamlike appearance. She gave the entire image a dark, muted green tone with the Color Balance command, and then applied the Blur More filter to the grass to give it more depth. Finally, to camouflage the banding that typically occurs with gradated images, she applied the Add Noise filter (set to 5) with the Gaussian method of distribution. f/x

Composite of original and manipulated carousel image.

**Artist:** Erik Adigard
**Image:** Medior
**Software:** Photoshop 3.0; Adobe Illustrator 3.0;
Ray Dream Designer 2.0

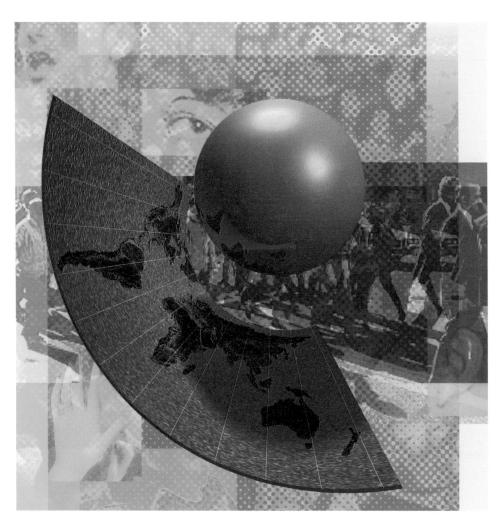

Erik Adigard is a San Francisco-area artist and illustrator, who, with his partner Patricia McShane, runs the design studio M.A.D. This image was done as one of a series in a brochure for the multimedia company Medior. Adigard began with a black-and-white stock photo that he scanned in Grayscale mode.

The original stock photo scanned in grayscale and colorized.

After opening the image in Photoshop, he switched to RGB mode and used Color Balance to make it bluish while still retaining some black. Next he duplicated the original grayscale scan and changed it into a bitmap, specifying a halftone screen frequency of 10 lines per inch, a screen angle of 45 degrees and a round dot shape. The idea was to make the photo look like a cross between a pattern and an image, similar to a newspaper halftone.

The bitmapped copy of the photo.

129

After pasting the bitmapped duplicate onto another layer, Adigard used Layer Options to specify Lighten mode at 5 percent opacity, selecting a small section of the RGB image and pasting it onto a layer positioned above the bitmapped layer so it would be unaffected by the bitmap layer; he repeated this process a number of times, selectively pasting and deselecting progressively larger parts of the images so that different areas would be affected in varying degrees.

The composite of the duplicate and the original after numerous selective pastes and the addition of other elements.

Adigard created the 3D globe and map objects in Ray Dream Designer, then brought them both into Photoshop, where he pasted them onto different layers and reduced their opacity to 10 percent, which made them just barely visible. Now he could see the position of the finished objects he would later bring in, and position the other elements around them since he didn't know until the end the size and opacity he wanted for them. In Hue/Saturation he changed the color of both objects to bright yellow so he could see them better. After bringing in all the other elements, which he'd previously scanned in grayscale, he pasted them onto another layer and used Layer Options to set Normal mode at 55 percent opacity. He colorized each of them with Hue/Saturation.

To further define the background, Adigard added color to various parts of the background using Hue/Saturation and Color Balance. He selected a small rectangular area in the top-right corner and filled it with a gradation from dark green at the bottom to white at the top in Lighten mode with 100 percent opacity—then boosted the green's saturation until it was just the shade he wanted.

Next Adigard scanned a color photo of people crossing a downtown street. He cropped it, intensified the colors and contrast, then pasted it in two steps: first he selected a geometric shape within the photo and pasted that into a layer in the right side of the background using Layer Options in Darken mode at 33 percent opacity.

Then he selected another geometric shape from the photo and pasted that into another layer in Normal mode at 44 percent opacity. He deliberately offset the second shape so that it only partially overlapped the first shape. To crank up the highlights, he repasted the second shape onto another layer using Lighten mode at 20 percent. On the left side of the image, he followed a similar process: he selected a different portion of the photo and did two successive pastes, using the same settings as he did for the second and third pastes on the right.

The background image with selections of the crosswalk photo pasted into it.

The map surface came from a clip-art collection; it was applied to the curved object in Ray Dream Designer. Once the object was imported into Photoshop, Adigard selected the water area, made the white gray by decreasing the brightness (Brightness/Contrast), then applied the Add Noise filter (set to 200) to the water to create the texture. After that, he applied the Motion Blur filter set Distance to 4.

Finally, he colorized the map with Color Balance. To create the contours of the map, he created a channel for the continents into which he pasted details from other scanned map images and colorized them. ▟

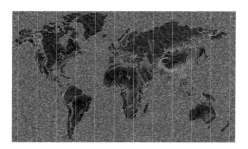

The finished map surface before it was mapped onto the 3D object.

**Artist:** Diane Fenster
**Image:** Talking Heads Revisited
**Software:** Photoshop 3.0; Specular Collage 1.01;
Terrazzo (beta version)

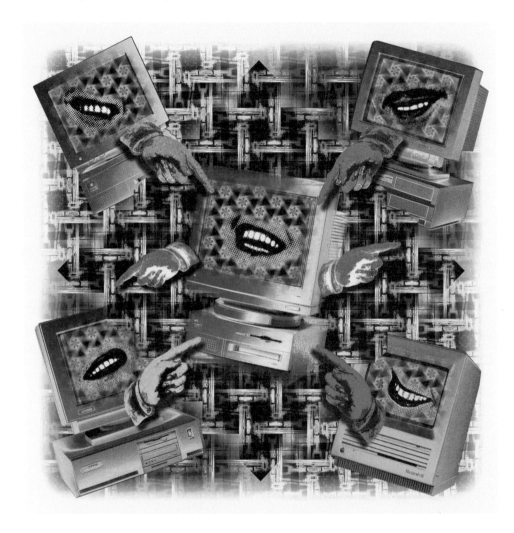

Fenster created this image for an article on networking that appeared in *InfoWorld* magazine. While trying to come up with a fresh new metaphor for networking that hadn't been used before, she applied Terrazzo, Xaos Tools's pattern generator, to a small section of one of her fine art images. Choosing the Pinwheel symmetry (one of 17 geometric shapes you can select in Terrazzo) produced a striking weavelike pattern—and the metaphor she was looking for.

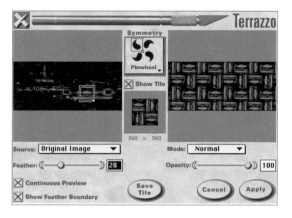

Terrazzo screen showing the section of art used to generate the first Terrazzo tile.

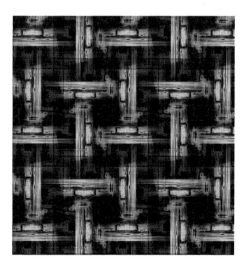

A section of the resulting Terrazzo pattern.

With the path tool, Fenster drew a rectangular path around the edges of the pattern and then a zigzag path in a diamond shape within the rectangle. After making that a selection (within the Paths palette), she selected Inverse and deleted the area around the zigzag diamond shape.

133

The diamond shape
with zigzag edges.

After drawing a triangular path adjacent to one side of the diamond, she made it a selection with a 35-pixel feather. Going back to the original background pattern, she copied it and pasted it into the selection; she repeated this process for the other three sides.

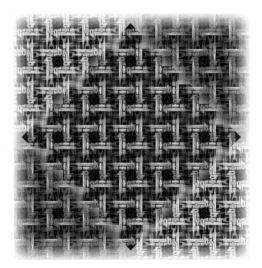

The diamond shape
with the four
corner selections.

For the top right and bottom left corners, Fenster altered the colors by decreasing the Hue to -101; for the top left and bottom right corners, she boosted the Hue to +160. After making another selection of the top left corner with no feather, she expanded the selection by holding down the shift key and dragging. Meanwhile, Fenster solarized (Filter>Stylize>Solarize) scanned photos of several different Macs and duplicated them.

The solarized Mac Quadra
with its original screen.

After outlining the copy as a selection, Fenster pasted it into each of the corner selections, so that each computer appeared to be tucked into the weave pattern, while the hard edge of the computers contrasted nicely with the soft feathered edge of the zigzag corners. After rotating and resizing each of the corner computers, she pasted another one in the center of the image, giving it a 15-pixel feather.

Because she wanted to replace the original computer screen with an-other Terrazzo pattern she'd created, Fenster made a selection of the screen using the lasso tool while holding down the option key to create straight lines. To remove the existing screen image, she used the eyedropper to click on a color she liked in the screen image, then option-clicked it to make it the background color. After feathering the selection 27 pixels, she copied the new Terrazzo pattern, defined it as a pattern (the Define Pattern command) and used the Fill command to fill the screen with the Terrazzo pattern; she repeated the process for each of the screens.

The mouths were scrap art from old advertisements that had large halftone dots. Using the lasso to select part of the mouth, she feathered it with a 7-pixel radius, then pasted, rotated and resized it. In the Hue/Saturation dialog box, she checked the Colorize option and increased the hue.

The original scanned
brass hand.

The hands were created from an antique brass hand Fenster had scanned in; she made four separate files and gave each one a different hue. Because she wanted to add some shadows to the hands—and because she wasn't sure exactly where she wanted to position them, she brought them into Collage for compositing. The entire image without the hands became the background layer in Collage; then the hands were brought in—each with its own mask, rotated, and shadows were applied. f/x

**Artist:** John Lund
**Image:** Rough Color
**Software:** Photoshop 3.0; Gallery Effects, Vol. 1

John Lund is a San Francisco-based photographer and photo-illustrator. Originally intended to be a stock photo, this image evolved into an illustrative piece for Lund's fine art portfolio. Lund took the original photo, a shot of workers—colloquially known as roughnecks—on an oil rig in the swamplands of Louisiana. Because he shot the photo on an overcast day, it started out as a rather flat, lackluster image without much color. So his objective was to heighten color, contrast and brightness—to give it a richly textured, illustrative look.

The original scanned photo.

Lund began by changing the color mode from RGB to CMYK—not to make color separations but because he wanted a black channel he could work on apart from the other channels; he often skips around from one channel to another, applying different filters to each to explore new ways of enhancing an image.

The image with Curves applied to the black channel.

In this case, he manipulated the Curves in the black channel to boost contrast and density. Then he used Gallery Effects's Spatter filter (Spray Radius set to 25; Smoothness set to 4) in the magenta channel.

137

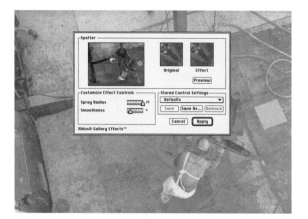

Applying Gallery Effects's Spatter filter to the magenta channel.

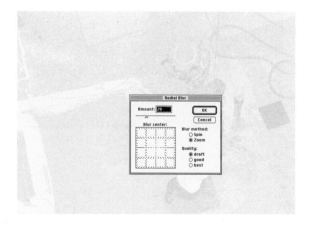

The image after the Spatter filter was applied.

Lund applied the Radial Blur filter in the yellow channel set to zoom (with Amount set to 28). In the CMYK channel he went into Hue/Saturation to heighten the Saturation to +50. Back in the black channel, he went into Brightness/Contrast, boosting Contrast to +44 and lowering Brightness to -5.

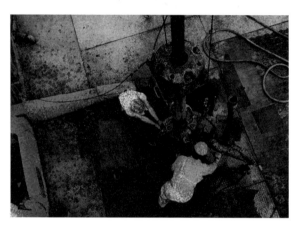

Applying the Radial Blur filter to the yellow channel.

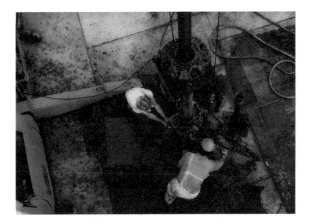

The image after increasing saturation in the CMYK channel.

After converting back to RGB mode (because the final output would be a transparency), he went into the RGB channel and adjusted highlights and midtones in the Color Balance window, dramatically increasing both the yellow and red levels to 75. fx

After brightness and contrast were adjusted in the black channel.

**Artist:** Nanette Wylde
**Image:** Exodus
**Software:** Photoshop 3.0

# An artist and illustrator based in Redwood City, California,

Nanette Wylde created this piece especially for this book. She began by scanning the keys in Grayscale mode at 150 dpi. After enlarging the canvas, she collaged the keys in an arrangement that would act as a border for the image.

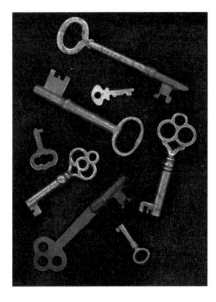

The original scan of the keys.

Next she applied the Emboss filter to the keys with the following settings: Angle: 45, Height: 5 pixels, Amount: 100 percent. After switching to RGB mode, she used Color Balance to set Midtones to +60 in the red channel, -10 in the green channel and -45 in the blue channel. To complete the effect, she boosted the Brightness to +40 and lowered the Contrast to -20.

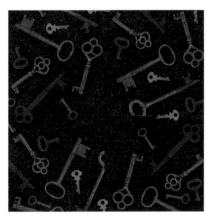

The keys after they were collaged.

141

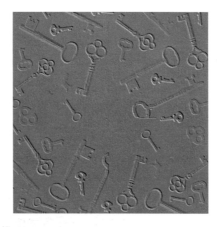

The keys after the Emboss filter was applied.

The moon image was a color scan of a photograph taken by Apollo 11 astronauts in July 1969, with stars added to provide an illusion of depth. Pasted on the embossed keys, this became the background layer.

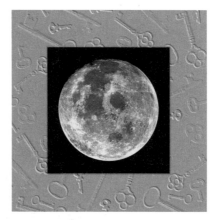

The moon pasted over the keys.

The butterfly images originated from a Magnetic Resonance Image (MRI) of the artist's own brain. She received the file as a 72-dpi grayscale TIFF measuring 3.5 by 3.5 inches.

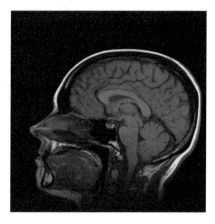

The original scan of the Magnetic Resonance Image (MRI).

After switching to RGB mode, she set Midtones to -80, +20 and +65 in the Color Balance dialog box. To get a translucent, outline effect, Wylde applied the Find Edges filter, which produced colors complementary to the colors in the original image. Because she wanted the image to be larger and at a higher resolution than the original, Wylde increased its size to 5 by 5 inches and upped the resolution to 150 dpi.

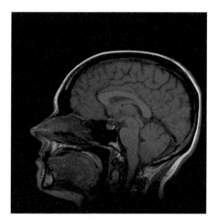

The scan of the brain with Color Balance applied.

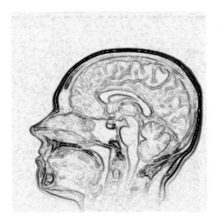

The brain scan after
the Find Edges filter
was applied.

To paste in the first wing, she erased the area around the skull image, and selected the white background with the magic wand with a feather of 5 pixels (to give the wing a slight halo when pasted) and copied it. After inversing the selection, she chose Paste Layer from the Edit menu to paste the wing onto another layer and then used the Layer Options to specify Normal mode and 85 percent opacity. Then she rotated it 60 degrees counterclockwise (CCW).

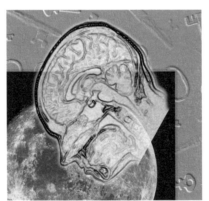

After the first wing was
added.

To create the second wing on top of the body, Wylde left a small margin (5 pixels) of the yellow background as she erased around the skull image. Again she pasted onto another layer, this time at 100 percent opacity. To give the top wing a vibrant translucency, she chose Remove White Matte (Select>Matting). The yellow margin created a translucent edge instead of a solid white edge after compositing. After rotating the wing 75 degrees CCW, Wylde used the blur tool to soften its edge.

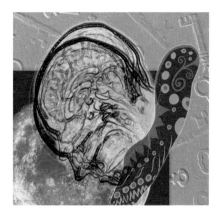

After the second wing
was added.

The body was painted in a separate document and pasted into
the moon. Wylde selected the background with the magic wand and
a 2-pixel feather, then inverted the selection, copied and pasted it
onto another layer.

To create the shadows, Wylde selected the body again, lowering
the Contrast to -100 to remove all the detail and leave just the shape
of the body in a solid gray. Pasting the body onto another layer she
double-clicked on the layer to bring up Layer Options. There she set
opacity to 50 percent, mode to Darken and the Underlying slider to
65 and 255. She adjusted the underlying images's color value range
so the shadows wouldn't show on the blue background behind the
moon. Wylde defringed the shadows by 2 pixels before deselecting,
then resized them with the Scale command. Edges were softened
with the blur tool. Once she was satisfied with the composition,
Wylde flattened the layers with the Flatten Image command on the
Layers palette. f/x

**Artist:** Kent Manske
**Image:** Conflict of Vision
**Software:** Photoshop 3.0; Fractal Design Painter 2.0

# Kent Manske, a Redwood City, California-based artist, likes to
combine different textures in his work. For this image, created especially for this book, he assembled a physical (as opposed to digital)
collage consisting of a wooden cross, some nails, a leaf, a circuit
board and a photo of sperm; then he scanned it into Photoshop.
Using the elliptical marquee, Manske selected a circular area of the
collage and pasted the circular cutout in the center of the eye.

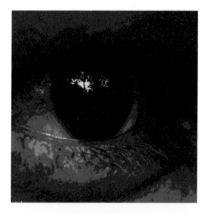

The posterized eye
scanned in grayscale.

The posterized collage
scan.

After scanning the photo of the four hands in grayscale, Manske
applied the Sharpen and Sharpen More filters. He posterized the
image to 5 levels of gray, then changed it into a bitmap so the
hands would have a different texture than the rest of the image, to
make them jump out of the image. However, bitmapped images that
are pasted into RGB images and then resized—as this one had to be
for publication in this book—lose their bitmap characteristics because
the bitmaps are converted into gray levels. For this reason, Manske
planned his final size and resolution early in the process: the finished image was originally a 300-dpi 20-by-20-inch Iris inkjet print
on BFK paper. Before cutting out the hands and pasting them into
the image, he dragged the rectangular marquee around the area he

147

planned to place them. Then he decreased the Brightness to -34 and upped the Contrast to +22. The point was to keep that part of the underlying image visible while making the pasted image stand out as well.

The posterized hand.

The bitmapped hand.

Next he posterized the eye while it was still in Grayscale mode. That way he could choose his own colors rather than take what too often turns out to be a bizarre color scheme that Photoshop comes up with during the posterization process. To create his color palette, Manske opened the Swatches floating palette (File>Palettes>Show Swatches). To remove all the default swatch colors, he loaded his custom palette of all white swatches to avoid being influenced by any preset colors, for the same reason a natural-media artist dislikes using oil paints straight from the tube. He then began mixing new colors using the toolbox's Color Picker (by double-clicking on the foreground color swatch in the toolbox) rather than the floating palette Color Picker, because the toolbox uses larger swatches. After mixing his colors, he kept the Swatches palette open to make sure the colors worked well in proximity to each other.

Once his color palette was complete, he used the magic wand to select an area, then chose Similar (Select menu) to select all other areas of the same level of gray, and used the Fill command (Edit) to fill it with the foreground color. He did this for each gray level until the eye was completely colorized.

The collage and hands pasted into the posterized eye image.

The eye image colorized.

To select the line art, which were his original brush-and-ink drawings, Manske used the magic wand with Tolerance set to 1 and the Anti-aliased box unchecked (to select only the line art without bringing in any fringe areas) and pasted it into the image.

Next, Manske placed a handmade piece of white paper, with a black piece of paper on top of it, on the scanner so that he could scan (in Grayscale mode) the paper's deckle, or uneven edge. After posterizing the deckle image, he increased the canvas size of the collage image and made the background black. This allowed him to lasso the whole deckle and paste it into the image. Because the black of the scan merged with the black of the image background, the seam between them disappeared.

The deckle scanned in grayscale.

At this point, Manske brought the illustration into Painter and applied a paper texture (Rough Paper from the Paper palette) to most of the background area, except for the deckle and the black outer edge, to create the illusion of a piece of paper against a black background.

Now here's how the artist turned adversity into creativity: in the course of developing this image, Manske accidentally shattered the glass door to his backyard as he went to find a leaf to add to his collage. As he swept up the shards of glass that littered the floor, he decided they'd add a nice effect to the piece, as well as a reminder of how they got there. So he scanned some of the shards, putting an off-white piece of paper over them to heighten the contrast on the edges of the glass.

The original scan of glass shards.

After posterizing the scan to 2 levels, he selected the black areas with the magic wand and copied them to the Clipboard. Reverting back to the original grayscale image, he posterized it again, this time to 5 levels. Then he pasted the Clipboard copy (the black areas) over the posterized glass image—which defined the edges of the glass—and deleted the lightest shade of gray (the dominant shade) so that only the edges were left.

The composite of the first and second posterizations.

Using the magic wand to select the white background, Manske used the Inverse command to select the dark edges. After copying the dark edges onto another layer he pasted them onto another layer and used Layer Options to set the opacity to 60 percent. Selecting the glass pieces with the lasso tool constrained (option-shift), so he could click from point to point to create straight lines, gave the illusion of thick edges on the glass. After filling the glass shards with the foreground color (black) at 12 percent opacity in Darken mode, he pasted more glass shards over some of the existing ones. To simulate the look of glass overlaying glass, he used the same fill with an 8 percent opacity, which made the overlapping glass areas slightly darker. To reduce the file size, he merged layers as he finished individual steps, flattening the image as the final step. ▨

**Artist:** Nance Paternoster
**Image:** ElizHdlndzSp
**Software:** Photoshop 3.0; Fractal Design Painter;
Gallery Effects, Vol. 1

In this piece, the artist started with a Polaroid close-up self-portrait that she scanned into Photoshop. She tinted the photo and then inverted the image (Image>Map>Invert) to make it look solarized. She then imported the image into Fractal Design Painter, where she painted around the borders of the photo with the chalk tools.

Original scan of face.

Inverted scan on background texture.

Paternoster also scanned sequential photos of a ballet dancer friend (to simulate photographer Eadweard Muybridge's motion-study sequences) and inverted their maps (Image>Map>Invert).

153

Opaque dancer.

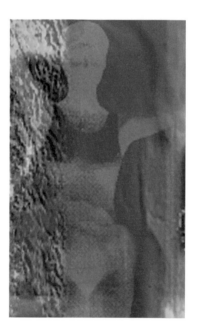

Inverted transparent dancer.

She applied the Color Halftone filter (Stylize>Color Halftone) to different versions and sizes of each photo.

Detail of area with Photoshop's Color Halftone filter applied.

In Photoshop, she used Gallery Effects's Color Embossing filter on various parts of the image. To simulate the effect of passing time and movement, she repasted the same image in different sizes with slightly different colors and textures—pasting into some selections and pasting behind others. *ƒx*

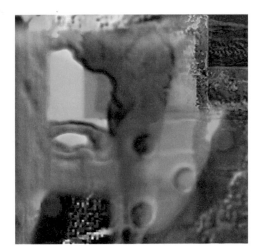

Face with Gallery Effects's Emboss filter applied.

**Artist:** Bonny Lhotka
**Image:** Eclipse
**Software:** Photoshop 3.0; Fractal Design Painter; Ofoto

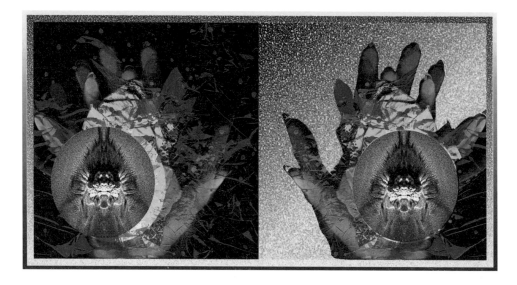

# Bonny Lhotka

is a Boulder, Colorado-based artist whose approach to making computer art is intuitive rather than planned. While working at the computer during the solar eclipse, she glanced out the window. The magical quality of the light, evoking a feeling of day and night simultaneously, inspired her to create this image.

Lhotka began by holding clear cellophane and strips of paint scraps and placing her hand on her three-pass scanner, draping a black cloth over her hand to block out the light. After each pass, she added or removed some of the objects. Keeping her hand very still during each pass while scanning at 100 dpi helped minimize blurring. She saved the image and set it aside to use later.

(1) The original scanned image.

Using the scanning software, Ofoto, she applied the balance exposure command and saved the new image.

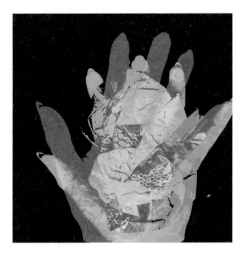

(2) After Ofoto's Balance Exposure command was applied to a copy of the first image.

In Photoshop, she used the magic wand tool to select the large black area in image 2. Using the gradient tool in Normal mode with a Linear fill and a Midpoint Skew of 50 percent, she replaced it with a bluish black.

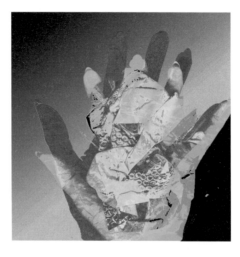

(3) After the gradient was applied to the second image.

Next she scanned in a photo of a rock in the sand at Venice beach that appeared to be facelike and sharpened the image twice.

Selecting half the image, she mirrored it to create the face. She boosted the Contrast (+10), and adjusted the Hue/Saturation and Color Balance controls (both -5). Then she brought the image into Painter, where she applied lighting to illuminate the face.

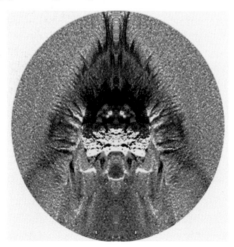

(4) The mirrored rock after applying color adjustments in Photoshop and lighting in Painter.

Reopening the original image, she intensified the Hue (+38) in the background from blue to purple. Then she used the elliptical marquee to select a circular area slightly larger than the face she'd just created and saved it as a mask. Image 5 was pasted on top of image 3 to create image 6.

(5) The original image after the background was changed to purple and the circular mask was created.

(6) The result of pasting image 5 over image 3.

The mask from image 3 was used again to drop out the same area on image 6 to return the gradient area that was in image 3. She applied the Pointillist filter set at cell size 5 to just the gradated upper-left portion.

(7) After the mask was used to bring in the gradation from image 3 and the Pointillist filter was applied.

The face image was then dropped in place leaving a fine eclipse-like halo. But Lhotka decided she preferred the vibrant blue background from the original scan. To get it, she pasted image 7 without the pointillized area over image 1. She again dropped in the face, offsetting it slightly to signify the passing of the eclipse.

(8) After the facelike rock was added.

(9) After the blue background was brought back (by pasting image 8 over image 1) and the face was dropped in and offset slightly.

To create the final composition, Lhotka changed the canvas size and flipped image 9, then added image 8. Borders were created by increasing the canvas size twice—a quarter-inch each time. For the inside border, she selected the area and applied the gradient tool (purple to green), then applied the Pointallize filter with cell size set at 3. To create the outer border, she increased the canvas size again, and applied the gradient tool, reversing the colors she'd used for the inner border. She boosted the Contrast to +10 to double the final image size without losing detail and flattening out the colors. f/x

**Artist:** John Lund
**Image:** Rainy City
**Software:** Photoshop 3.0; Gallery Effects, Vol. 1

This image was used in an advertisement for a water-management system. Lund began by scanning in a photo of a dark sky.

The original scan of the dark sky.

The clouds in the image, however, lacked definition. So he opened a scan of another photo with fluffy white clouds and used the cropping tool to crop out a section for use as a mask.

The cropped scan of the second cloud image.

Back in the original cloud image, he opened a new channel into which he pasted the second cloud image. After loading the selection, he went into the Brightness/Contrast dialog box, where he set Contrast to +30 and Brightness to +100.

The mask created from the second cloud image.

In another channel filled with black, he opened Gallery Effects and applied its Graphic Pen filter with the following settings: 15 for Stroke Length, Right Diag. for Stroke Direction, 16 for Light/Dark Balance. Then it was back to the RGB channel, where he adjusted the Curves (with Input at 190 and Output at 119) to darken the modified cloud image.

The modified sky with the cloud channel applied.

Now he was ready to add the hammock, a photo he'd taken with the Leaf Digital Camera. Selecting it with the magic wand tool, he copied and pasted it into the modified cloud image and saved the selection.

The skyline was a scanned 35mm slide he'd taken of San Francisco's financial district. After using the rubber stamp tool's Clone options to beef up the skyline and cover up unsightly billboards, he drew a path around the buildings with the pen tool and saved the path.

The skyline after buildings were added and signs removed.

To simulate a stormy day, he set Brightness to -35 and Contrast to -15, which darkened the buildings and decreased the overall contrast. He copied and pasted the city skyline behind the hammock, holding down the option key while choosing Paste Into, then saved the selection into a new alpha channel.

Finally, he loaded the rain selection previously created with Gallery Effects's Graphic Pen filter and applied +100 Brightness and -50 Contrast to get the rain just right.

The rain mask created with Gallery Effects's Graphic Pen filter.

Lund created yet another channel and used the gradient tool to fill it with a gradation of white at the top and black at the bottom. Once he'd loaded the selection, he went back to the RGB channel and in the Brightness/Contrast dialog box moved the Brightness slider to -30 to darken the upper part of the image.

Lund painted the lightening in with very small airbrushes in white using successively thicker brushes: he started at the top with a 3-pixel brush, then 2-pixel, then finished with a 1-pixel brush. f/x

**Artist:** Patricia McShane
**Image:** Road Dream
**Software:** Photoshop 3.0

# Patricia McShane is a San Francisco Bay area artist and illustrator who shares M.A.D. Studio with her partner Erik Adigard. She did this illustration to accompany a *Ray Gun* magazine article in which members of different rock bands were asked what they've dreamed about while on the road.

McShane scanned a baby mask—one of many unique objects that can be found in their studio—and changed it to blue with the Hue/Saturation command. Then she pasted each version on a separate layer and used Layer Options to change the mode to Lighten.

The baby masks after they were duplicated and colorized.

Next she scanned a photo taken by L. Calsoni of two rather bizarre images: a mannequin wearing some strange head gear, and a headless Barbie doll in an antique meat grinder; each was used as a separate element in the illustration. After using the Spherize filter to distort the mannequin's head, she silhouetted it, copied and pasted it into the image of the babies with a light feather edge.

Next she scanned another object in the studio, an inflatable clown, and in the Brightness/Contrast dialog box cranked up the contrast as high as it would go. After changing the colors with the Hue/Saturation command, she pasted the clown image onto a new layer and changed to Darken mode in Layer Options. This made the blue baby masks show through and mix with the yellow of the clown's ears, transforming his ears into a glowing lime green.

The clown after the colors were manipulated with the Hue/Saturation and Brightness/Contrast commands.

Next the headless Barbie doll was cropped from the original scan; McShane used the Colorize option in Hue/Saturation to give it a duotone effect. Then she stretched the doll with the Perspective command (Image> Effects>Perspective). Next she drew an oval and stroked it with 16 pixels on the inside of the oval, so she could select it without losing any of the stroke. She copied and pasted it into the composition.

The Barbie doll colorized and stretched in perspective.

For the background, McShane scanned a slide of a wheat field, then used Hue/Saturation to make the sky chartreuse. To create a surreal, dreamlike effect, she selected the wheat field, went into the red channel and moved the selection just a few pixels so it would be slightly out of register, then boosted the contrast.

A section of the wheat field before and after manipulation.

After compositing the mannequin, the Barbie doll in the oval, the babies and the clown, McShane made a mask using the oval tool to create a series of overlapping ovals, some with a 32-pixel feather and others with no feather. Finally, she loaded the selection, copied it and pasted it over the field. f/x

All the objects composited into one image.

The mask created from the overlapping oval shapes.

**Artist:** Ruth Kedar
**Image:** Rose Whirl
**Software:** Photoshop 3.0

For this fine art piece, Kedar began by scanning an old menu from a cruise ship. After duplicating the background layer and naming it Texture, she selected a small section of the menu and enlarged it to fill the whole canvas, then applied the Median filter with a 10-pixel radius. To this layer she applied Photoshop's Add Noise filter using the Gaussian option and a value of 300 and checked the Monochromatic box, which produced a very dense texture. In Layer Options, she selected Difference mode with 80 percent opacity and deselected.

The original menu scan.

Enlarged section of menu with Median and Add Noise filters applied.

Next Kedar created a new channel in which she drew a rectangle along the left third of the area and filled it with white. Using the lasso tool with a 30-pixel feather, she softened the right vertical edge and gave it a ragged, irregular edge that blended between white and black. Then she selected all, inverted the colors (Image>Map>Invert) and copied.

171

The next step was combining the original menu image with the newly created Texture layer. In the Layers palette, Kedar added a layer mask to the Texture layer and pasted the channel (of the ragged, irregular edge) she had just copied. This composited the original menu scan through the ragged-edge mask.

Original menu and
enlarged manipulated
texture composited
through the blend mask.

Creating a duplicate (Image>Duplicate), which she called Twirl, Kedar checked the Merged Layers Only box. After rotating the new Twirl image 90 degrees clockwise, she applied the Twirl filter at 160 degrees and inverted the colors. Next she opened channel #4, pasted the original brooch scan into it and boosted the Contrast to +42. With the magic wand and a 5-pixel-radius feather, she selected the area around the brooch, and filled it with black. Then she selected all and copied.

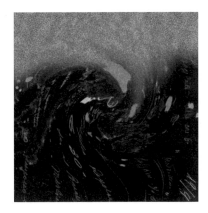

Menu/Texture Composite rotated, twirled, inverted and saved as Twirl.

After creating a new layer called Brooch, Kedar pasted, then added a layer mask. In the mask, she used the gradient tool to create a diagonal blend from the top right to the center, which allowed the background to show through at varying degrees. f/x

The original scan of the brooch.

Channel with the brooch pasted in, contrast heightened and feathered background filled with black.

**Artist:** Nance Paternoster
**Image:** Herb
**Software:** Photoshop 3.0

**Herb is one** of a series of drawings about healing one's body that the artist did after she spent a long time recuperating from a motorcycle accident by using acupuncture and Chinese herbs. She composited a figure she'd drawn in pencil and charcoal with textures from Chinese herbal packaging labels.

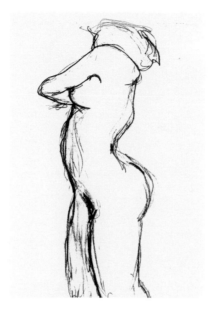

The original scan of the figure drawing.

The scans from the Chinese herb packaging.

After making a selection within the figure, she pasted various parts of the same herb-package texture into the selection. As she pasted, she kept the selection active and used the scale tool to enlarge various parts of the packaging to different sizes. She then did the same for the background.

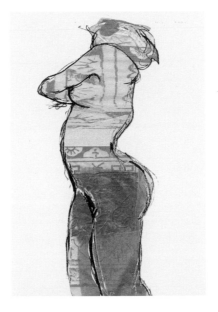

Various parts of the herb-package texture pasted into the figure.

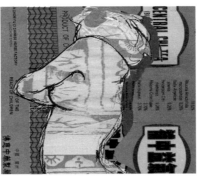

Various parts of the texture pasted into the background.

Because the original box had folds in it, Paternoster used the rubber stamp tool with the Non-aligned option to paint away the folds. With the same texture she used for the background still selected in another document, she loaded the saved selection of the figure and pasted it onto a new layer. To create the shadow behind the figure, she loaded the original selection of the figure (background layer) and then pasted the green texture into the figure. While the figure was still selected, she darkened the selection.

After the rubber stamp tool was used to paint out the folds in the box.

She again selected the figure with the textures, moving it up and to the left to complete the shadow. Using Terrazzo, she generated some additional patterns, which she pasted onto layers above the background with varying levels of transparency. To generate the patterns, she used an image she'd created in a 3D program and a chicken image from one of the herb packages as the other. On the chicken image, she used Terrazzo's Turnstile symmetry in Normal mode at 41 percent opacity and pasted it over the background at 55 percent opacity. On the 3D image, she used the tile option in Multiply mode at 35 percent opacity. f/x

The patterns applied to the image.

**Artist:** Ruth Kedar
**Image:** 2050
**Software:** Photoshop 3.0; Kai's Power Tools 2.0;
Andromeda Filters, Series 1 and 2

This image was done for the artist's fine art portfolio. She opened a scanned color photo of her son, duplicated the background layer and named the new layer Fangs, which she colorized in Photoshop. With a 10-pixel feather, she selected the hair with the lasso and altered the color by setting Saturation to 100 while leaving both Hue and Lightness at the default setting of zero. Selecting the face with the lasso, she filled it (Edit>Fill) with a green at 100 percent opacity in Color mode. Using a feathered oval selection, she filled the eyes with white, then drew the fangs with the brush tool.

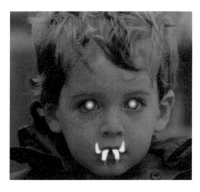

The Fangs layer after different areas were selected and colorized and fangs were added.

To the Fangs layer Kedar added a layer mask. In the Channels palette, she hid all but the layer mask. Making a rectangular selection on the left quarter of the image, she filled it with a black-to-white gradation, selected Inverse and made a white-to-black gradation. After selecting the left half of the image, she option-dragged to the right half to create four gradations and then deselected.

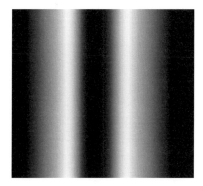

The layer mask with four parallel gradations.

This enabled the mask to determine which areas of the two layers would show through and the degree to which they would be visible. Kedar saved the result to a new file called Colorized Image.

Going back to the original scan, Kedar converted it first to grayscale, then to bitmap using Diffusion Dither. She copied and pasted the bitmapped image into a new layer in the file Colorized Image. Naming the layer Mezzo, she set its opacity to 63 percent in Hard Light mode and grouped it with the previous layer so that the Mezzo layer would only show through the layer mask. Then she flattened the image.

The bitmapped image pasted onto the Mezzo layer with the layer mask applied.

With a 5-pixel feather, Kedar made a horizontal selection across the eyes and applied Color Curves to get a psychedelic effect. After setting the background color to black, she enlarged the canvas size to create a border around the image. Then she selected the left section of the face and moved it down. To invert everything except the center selection, she used the Inverse command (Select menu) and then the Invert command (Image>Map). At this point, Kedar had a finished image, which become part of her "mask" series. But she continued manipulating the face to generate the final image you see here.

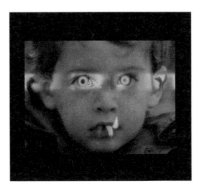

After a horizontal section across the eyes was manipulated with Image>Adjust>Curves and one vertical section was shifted down.

The image was inverted except for the vertical section.

Next she applied 3D Noise good one, a preset texture from KPT Texture Explorer, to the entire image. The result was an unusual texture that bore no resemblance to its original source. Selecting a vertical section in the center of the new image, she inverted the side sections to black. Using the Andromeda 3D filter, she wrapped the image onto a long, narrow cylindrical shape, rotating the image at an angle so that it was not parallel to the cylinder, to get a distorted effect. Kedar then went back to the texture she'd created and used the same Andromeda filter—this time wrapping it around a short, wide cylinder. Selecting both cylinders, she pasted them into a new file, and applied the Andromeda Series 1 Star filter to the narrow cylinder. f/x

KPT Texture Explorer (preset texture 3D Noise good one) applied to image.

Andromeda 3D filter applied to entire image and mapped onto a wide cylinder.

**Artist:** Nance Paternoster
**Image:** ChiOilFig
**Software:** Photoshop 3.0; Fractal Design Painter 2.0

Paternoster began by scanning into Photoshop a black-and-white drawing she'd done of a woman's figure. In Painter she used various brushes to create another image which was a graduated-color background with purples, yellows and greens. To make the liquidlike swirls, she used Painter's Apply Marbling option (Effects>Esoterica).

The original scanned black-and-white drawing.

Still in Painter, Paternoster applied the Glass Distortion filter to the whole composition and added lighting to generate the cylindrical peaks in color. She brought the image into Photoshop, and using the Painter image as her background, she made a selection of just the black-and-white figure from the original drawing and pasted that on a new layer above the Painter background. Then she applied a Mezzotint filter with the Fine settings option to give the black-and-white drawing a coarse texture.

The
background
generated and
distorted in
Painter.

The figure
added as a
new layer in
Photoshop.

She then applied a Gaussian Blur filter to the border of the background and darkened it a little with the Brightness/Contrast command. Opening the scanned Chinese herbal box in Photoshop, she pasted that into a new layer at 65 percent opacity to superimpose the scan on the image.

The Chinese herb box scanned into Photoshop.

YIN CHIAO CHIEH TU PIEN is made from 100% natural Chinese herbs. This traditional Chinese herbal mixture has long been a favorite among the Chinese and is now becoming quite popular abroad as well. This product was manufactured under antiseptic conditions and meets the strict standards of the Health Dept. of The People's Republic of China.

The herb box added to the composition as a new layer.

After copying the entire image and pasting it on a new layer, Paternoster adjusted the hue to give the colors a bright metallic effect. Back in Painter, she applied the Glass Distortion filter to the entire image, then imported it back into Photoshop onto a new layer and composited the two layers at 45 percent opacity. **f/x**

**Artist:** Nance Paternoster
**Image:** Pedi
**Software:** Photoshop 3.0; Infini-D 2.0; Gallery
Effects, Vol. 1; Paint Alchemy 1.0; Terrazzo 1.0

Paternoster began this image by scanning in one of her pen-and-ink drawings. She then created another image to use as a texture to apply to the figure's body. She started with a pastel gradation and used the finger tool to smear the color into different shapes.

The original scan of a pen-and-ink drawing by the artist.

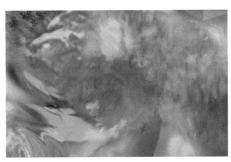

The texure she used for the figure's body.

She created another texture for the figure by making a dark blue-to-pastel gradation; to this texture she applied Paint Alchemy using the Weave Thatch Brush with the following settings: Vary Brush Transparency by vertical position, Top 21, Bottom 49 and Variation 59. Then she used Photoshop's Variations command to increase the saturation and add more blue to the texture.

187

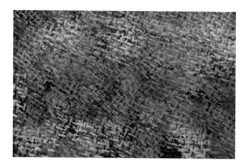

The Paint Alchemy
texture.

Next she selected the cloud areas and gave them a gold-to-red gradated fill. After applying the Add Noise filter (set to 45) to the clouds and the horizontal bands on the ground, she used the Gallery Effects Volume 1 Dry Brush filter just on the clouds. After selecting all the spots on the figure's torso, Paternoster pasted in the Paint Alchemy texture. For the torso itself, she used the original texture.

After various filters
were applied and the
Paint Alchemy texture
was added to the
figure.

The light cyan texture under the figure's feet was made by adjusting the colors of the Paint Alchemy texture using the Hue/Saturation command. Next she selected the white cubes in the shape to the right of the figure and pasted a small drawing she'd done of light- and dark-green concentric circles.

After the texture was added to the area beneath the feet and the concentric circles were pasted into the white cubes in the irregular shape.

After making another texture and pasting it into the black cubes within the shape, she made the whole shape a selection using the pen tool and generated a new color range. The next texture was a tile Paternoster generated in Terrazzo from a rendered 3D image.

After another texture was pasted into the black cubes.

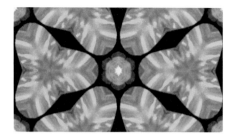

The first Terrazzo tile pattern.

To create the texture for the figure's pants, Paternoster first painted some colors onto a white background and then used Terrazzo's Crab Claws symmetry to generate the repetitive shiny pattern. To retain the lines of the sketch underneath the texture, she pasted that texture into the pants selection on the original image at 75 percent opacity in Normal mode. The first Terrazzo pattern was pasted into the triangular platform under the feet at an opacity of 55 percent.

The second Terrazzo pattern.

The rectangular shape to the left of the figure was created by making a rectangular selection and then applying the perspective (Image>Effect> Perspective) and rotating it. Then she gave it a graduated fill from light blue to light green. She copied the selection and applied the Distort effect to make the reflection. Then she applied a Gaussian Blur set to 4. After darkening it with Brightness/Contrast, she repasted the image into the area reflecting the figure's feet. Copying the other reflections from the platform above the green graduated fill, she pasted them into the area below and applied the scale effect and Gaussian Blur.

After the Terrazzo patterns were pasted into the image.

Paternoster generated the reflection of the shape on the right by copying the original and pasting it into the preselected white squares of the reflection shape. With this area still selected, she used the Twirl filter set to -210. To make the edges of the selection, she selected a single square of the original shape, defined it as a pattern and filled in the area with the pattern at 100 percent opacity. She pasted the hair texture at 85 percent opacity (using the Paint Alchemy texture generated earlier) and darkened it by adjusting the Contrast/Brightness. The final texture was generated in Infini-D 2.0. Then, the texture she painted for step 2 was used as a texture map and was wrapped onto all these models which she then rendered. f/x

After the shape's reflection was made and the hair texture was pasted in.

The 3D texture created in Infini-D.

**Artist:** Ruth Kedar
**Image:** Desert Winds 2
**Software:** Photoshop 3.0; Adobe Dimensions 2.0;
Andromeda Filters, Series 1

For this fine art piece, second in a series of six, Kedar began by scanning an old menu from a cruise ship of the 1940s. Then she duplicated the background layer and named it Manuscript. While working on that layer, she hid the background layer. To alter the shape and perspective of the menu, Kedar applied Photoshop's Skew and Distort commands (Image>Effects) to the Manuscript layer. To create an irregular edge, she used the Wave filter (Filter>Distort), setting the number of wave generators to 2, wave type to Sine (a rolling wave), and the Randomize option (defaults were used for all other settings).

Distorted menu with Wave filter applied.

Next Kedar selected the white background around the distorted menu with the magic wand and saved it as a selection (Distorted Selection channel). In the RGB channel she selected all, copied and created a new channel into which she pasted and inverted the selection. She manipulated the channel using the Levels command and Brightness/Contrast (with Brightness set to -18 and Contrast to +34) and saved the result as Highlights channel, then deselected.

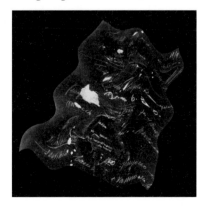

A new channel with the distorted menu selection inverted.

After going back to RGB mode, she deleted the Manuscript layer and selected the background layer. After loading the Distorted Selection channel, she darkened the selection with Levels, applied a 15-pixel feather and moved the selection down and to the right. Filling the selection with white completed the effect—a shadow along the right and bottom edges of the image. Next she loaded the Highlights channel and filled that selection with white also. The result was saved as a new file, called Parchment.

Finished image of manipulated menu saved as Parchment file.

The three-dimensional bottle, which Kedar had previously created in Adobe Dimensions (see Chapter 3 for a description of how it was done) was placed in Photoshop and rotated. After pasting it into the Parchment image, she applied the Andromeda Velocity filter just to the bottle itself.

Rotated bottle with parchment background and Andromeda Series 1 Velocity filter applied.

Then, to create a new texture, she went back to the original, undistorted menu scan file. This time, Kedar applied the Wave filter, specifying 10 wave generators, Triangle for wave type, and chose the Randomize option. In Image Size, she resized the texture to 150 percent (keeping its proportions intact) and applied Photoshop's Tiles (Filter>Stylize) filter, setting number of tiles to the maximum (99) at an offset of 60 percent. Then she selected all and copied.

Enlarged texture with Photoshop's Tile filter applied.

Activating the Parchment file, Kedar pasted the tiled texture onto a new layer called Tile, then deselected. After adding a layer mask containing a diagonal gradient, she set the mode to Multiply and opacity to 75 percent in Layer Options. f/x

Layer mask containing a diagonal gradient selection.

Tiled texture pasted onto the bottle through a gradient layer mask.

**Artist:** Marc Yankus
**Image:** Robeegraffix
**Software:** Photoshop 3.0; Kai's Power Tools 2.0

# Marc Yankus is an artist and illustrator based in New York
City. For this image, he started with a scanned photo of a space
background. He brought an EPS file of zeroes and ones into
Photoshop and put that on a layer. Then he filled it with color and
slightly blurred it.

The scanned photo of a space scene.

The scanned image of ones and zeroes.

Next Yankus brought in a marble texture from an Art Beats CD-ROM collection and made that the third layer; he used the KPT Glass Lens distort filter to make the texture into an orb shape.

The marble texture turned into an orb with KPT's Glass Lens filter.

On the fourth layer he placed a silhouetted square with a cloud texture from Page Overtures (another CD-ROM of textures) pasted into it.

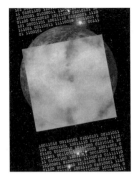

After the cloud image in the square was added.

After reducing the square's opacity to 70 percent and rotating it, Yankus scanned in a photo of a computer, then selected the monitor and pasted the cloud image and the orb image into it. Then he duplicated the computer and put each one on a different layer. One by one he rotated each computer layer, positioning them by eye to make them equidistant to each other around the orb.

The image with the computers added and rotated into place.

Yankus rotated the man until his head touched the sky and his feet touched the bottom of one of the computers. Next he added two more arms—each on its own layer, and did the same for the two extra legs.

After the figure of the man was added to the mix.

After the second set of arms were added—each on a separate layer.

To make part of the left leg transparent, Yankus added a layer mask, which he filled with a gradation (black to white: 100 percent transparent to 100 percent opaque). Dragging from the top to the middle of the leg, he made the top part of the extra legs slowly fade away, so they would blend seamlessly with the original, then used the same technique for the extra arms and head. f/x

After the extra legs were added—again on separate layers.

After the two additional heads were added.

**Artist:** Don Day
**Image:** The Issue at Hand
**Software:** Photoshop 3.0

For this image, Day began by opening an image he called "Full Fire," which automatically became the background layer. Dragging that layer to the New Layer icon created a Background Copy layer on top of the original background. On the copy layer, he used Color Range to select the black background; then he deleted it to make it transparent. Next he opened the file he called "Vertical Fire" and, using the move tool, dragged and dropped it onto the "Full Fire" image to create a new layer, sandwiching it between the original and the copy of the background image.

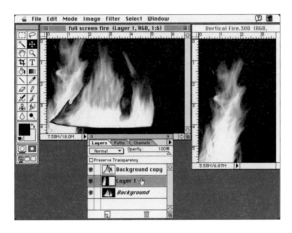

The original fire image with a layer added.

Closing "Vertical Fire," he opened another fire image, "Vertical Fire-rt" and used Color Range to select its background. After inversing the selection, he dragged the selection to "Full Fire" to create a floating selection. There, he scaled it, flipped it horizontally and repositioned it, then dragged it to the New Layer icon to create Layer 2. After saving a copy as "Full Screen Fire 2 Copy" he flattened it to create the final fire image.

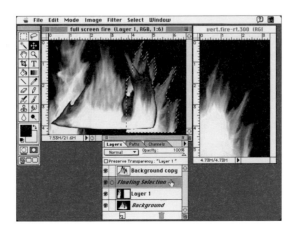

A new fire image selection being dragged and dropped onto the original fire.

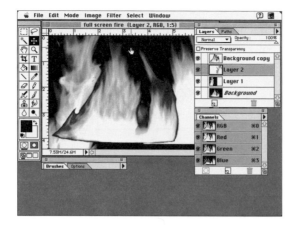

The fire with additional layers and the Background Copy.

The final fire image.

Next, Day opened the grayscale wave file, which he changed to RGB mode and made into a layer by double-clicking on it. Then he added a layer mask so that he could save a selection to it later. In Curves, he colorized the image by giving it blue tones. In the Color Range dialog box, he selected Highlights to select just the lighter areas of the wave. Choosing a new foreground color, he applied a fill in Color mode.

The original grayscale wave image.

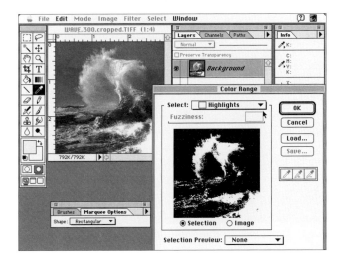

Selecting the wave's highlights with the Color Range command.

Using the dodge/burn/sponge tool with a brush size of 100 and 15 percent opacity, he burned in highlights in the lower-right corner to add slight gray values to the white areas. Using the foreground color, he again applied a fill in Color mode, saving the selection as "Wave.300.RGB." Using Color Range again, he selected the sky area; then, because Color Range also selected some areas of the water (below the skyline) that he didn't want, he deselected the water by holding the command key while using the lasso tool. After saving the selection as a layer mask on the background, he reopened the "Wave.300.RGB" file, clicked on the layer mask and inversed the selection.

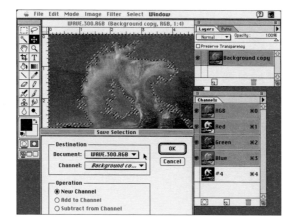

Saving the wave
selection as a
layer mask.

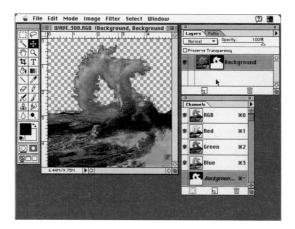

The inversed
layer mask.

Going back to "Full Screen Fire 2 copy, he selected all and
copied, then clicked on "Wave.300.RGB" and pasted the layer.
After positioning the fire image as the top layer, he saved it as
"Wave.SkyFire."

The wave
and the fire
layers with
the wave
layer mask.

The final wave/fire
composite.

The arm was pasted on a new layer, rotated and positioned
over the hole in the wave. To create the effect of the arm coming
out of the wave, Day used the gradient tool to create a blend in a
layer mask. f/x

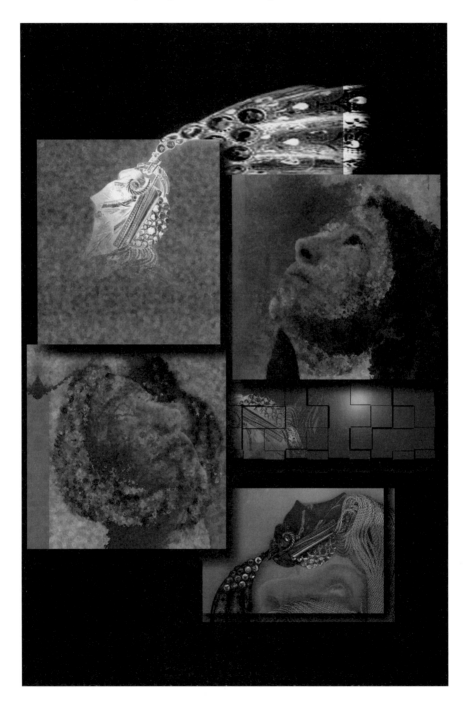

For this image, the artist scanned in a photo of herself in profile. Double-clicking on the layer to bring up Layer Options, she made the background into a layer so that she could add a layer mask to it. She then named it "Soft Profile." With the Soft Profile layer selected, Kedar applied the Paint Alchemy filter Sponge Print. After copying that layer, she used the Add Layer Mask and Paste commands to put the contents of the layer into the new layer mask. Now she had a grayscale version of the layer as a layer mask associated with the Soft Profile layer.

The Soft Profile layer with the Paint Alchemy filter applied.

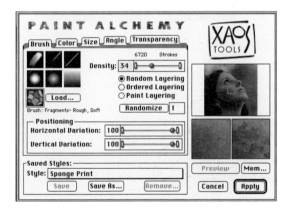

The Paint Alchemy dialog box with Sponge Print settings.

Next Kedar activated the Channels palette and made only the layer mask visible. With the magic wand, she selected the midtone values. With the selection still active, she created a black-to-white diagonal linear blend from the top right to the bottom left.

The mask area selected with the magic wand.

The layer mask after the diagonal linear blend was applied.

After opening the scanned image of a necklace, Kedar applied Paint Alchemy's Sponge Print—with the same settings she'd used earlier on the profile image—to the center of the necklace image. She selected all, copied  and pasted it into a new layer in the origi-nal file, then positioned the layer with the necklace under the Soft Profile layer and called it Background.

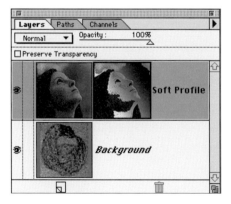

The Layers palette showing the background layer (with the necklace on it), the Soft Profile layer and the layer mask.

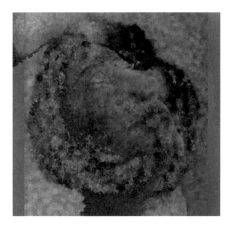

The effect created by the two layers and the layer mask.

On the Layers palette, she selected the layer mask—the same one she'd previously applied to the profile—and inverted it. Inverting the layer mask and reapplying it made different areas of the necklace scan show through the mask, allowing the artist to create an effect with as many different variations as possible. [f/x]

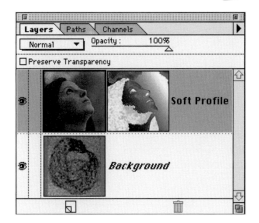

The Layers palette with the inverted mask shown.

# Richard Tuschman is a photo-illustrator based in Pearl River,

New York. This image was done for a book cover. Tuschman began with a background of surfaces he had painted traditionally and scanned in Grayscale mode. He marqueed the right half of the image and lightened it with Curves, then saved the selection to an alpha channel (which he called Split Mask). Because he wasn't satisfied with the first surface, he decided to combine it with another surface, which he put on another layer.

First background with right half lightened.

He made a feathered oval selection with the elliptical marquee, then saved that to another alpha channel (Vignette Mask). After loading the Split Mask selection into the Vignette Mask channel, he chose Inverse and used the Delete key to remove the left half of the Vignette Mask. In the black channel of the second layer, he loaded the remaining half of the Vignette Mask. To give the image a negative, glowing effect, he used the Invert command, then composited the two surfaces with Layer Options by setting each to 50 percent opacity. Then he flattened the layers.

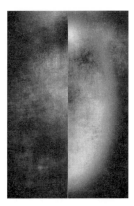

Second background with elliptical mask loaded and image inverted.

Because he wanted the central image of the two faces to stand out from the background, Tuschman created another background on which to put the faces by reducing the finished background to about half its original size and saving that to a separate file. Then he opened and resized the file with the woman's face, which he had previously composited from several different photos, and made a feathered selection of her face (15-pixel feather), saving that selection.

The feathered selection of the woman's face.

Using Layer Options, he pasted the face selection on the small background in Screen mode at 100 percent opacity. (He often uses Screen mode because it produces a translucent effect with the underlying image showing through, even at full opacity.) After deselecting it, he used the rectangular marquee tool to select the pasted face and floated that selection (Command-j), to which he applied the Gaussian Blue filter at about 4 pixels. He pasted the selection over the original at 80 percent opacity in Normal mode. Next he repasted the original face on top of the new composite and set Layer Options to 45 percent opacity to give it more definition, then deselected it and took a snapshot of the result. Using the rubber stamp tool, he alternated between the From Saved and From Snapshot options so he could selectively combine elements of both versions of the face.

The woman's face after it was pasted onto the background in Screen mode.

To get the old-fashioned-looking border around the central image, Tuschman scanned in a Polaroid photo against a black background to get a strongly defined edge, then resized it to match the rectangular shape of the face image and saved it to an alpha channel and aligned the two. He loaded the selection and copied and pasted it onto the main image (the background) and saved that.

The original scan of the man's face.

Next he resized the man's face to match the woman's face, made a feathered selection of about 20 pixels and pasted that on the main image, deselecting half the face with the marquee. With the face still a floating selection, he inverted it to give it a negative effect, set opacity to 65 percent in Layer Options and deselected.

To create the burned edge of the photo, he burned a piece of paper and scanned it, selected the paper and filled it with black. With the lasso, he selected just the part he wanted to use as a mask, copied it and pasted it into a new channel, then aligned it with the photo border. Going back to the main channel, he loaded the burned paper selection, and used the airbrush to darken the burnt edges. After inversing the selection, he used the rubber stamp to paint away the edges of the Polaroid photo by cloning the background underneath.

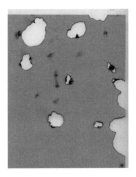

The scan of the burned paper.

To create the fire, he scanned in a crumpled piece of Saran wrap, applied Gaussian Blur at about 6 pixels and used the lasso tool with a 10-pixel feather to select the area that looked most flamelike. He pasted that on the main image and deselected it.

The two faces composited on the background with the burned paper.

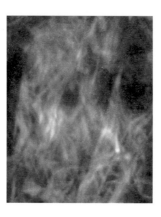

The flamelike crumpled Saran wrap.

Next Tuschman scanned in two photos of fake birds: a dark and a light one. He made masks for both by duplicating the image and saving that to an alpha channel; using Levels, he increased the contrast to make light gray areas white and dark gray areas black. He loaded the selection, copied it and pasted it onto the main image. Some of the birds were pasted behind the central image (by holding down the option key while choosing Paste Into); they were all pasted at 60 percent opacity, then resized and rotated.

The scan of the fake white bird.

The scan of the fake dark bird.

At this point, Tuschman was ready to colorize the image. He made a copy of the file and then he reduced the resolution from 300 dpi to 75 dpi so he could paint quickly with large brushes. Switching to RGB, he used the airbrush in Color mode at about 10 percent opacity. To differentiate the photo from the background, he loaded the photo selection so he could paint through the mask. To bring it up to high-res, he converted to Lab mode and resized it to exactly match the original by going into Image Size, unchecking Constrain Proportions, changing Height and Width from inches to pixels. The next step was to combine the light and dark values of the original high-res grayscale image with the color values of the color image. That was accomplished by first converting the grayscale version to Lab. Then, activating the Lightness channel in the color image, he chose Apply Image (Image menu) with the grayscale file as the source, Lightness as the channel and the color image and Lightness channel as the target. After compositing the two images, he converted back to RGB mode. f/x

**Artist:** Sigi Torinus
**Image:** Enchanted Vision
**Software:** Photoshop 3.0, Kai's Power Tools 2.0,
Paint Alchemy 1.0

Sigi Torinus is a San Francisco artist and illustrator. This fine art piece, about vision being obliterated, was originally designed as two rough images she later decided to merge into one. She began by scanning a number of black-and-white photographs in Grayscale mode, an eighteenth-century etching, two video captures and a flower.

Original scan of black-and-white photo of figure.

First she composited the black-and-white scans according to a compositional sketch she had previously made, creating an alpha channel for each element so she could select them individually. She then converted from grayscale to RGB. For each of the black-and-white images, she assigned colors—first using the Color Picker, then the Fill command in Color mode at 50 percent opacity. She made further color adjustments with the Color Balance and Hue/Saturation commands.

Going back to the original black-and-white images, she copied selected parts of the black-and-white imagery and pasted them onto different layers using Layer Options to vary the modes and opacity levels (between 30 percent and 50 percent). To simulate depth of field, she applied the Gaussian Blur filter set at 5–10 pixels to the image's background elements, then added a blue tone by adjusting blue midtones and shadows (Image>Adjust>Color Balance) to the architectural elements in the background, and contrast (Image>Adjust) to the the video images within the floating rectangle. To blend the edge where one image ended and the next one began, she selected the "seam" and applied one or another of the following distortion filters: Wave, Ripple and Zigzag.

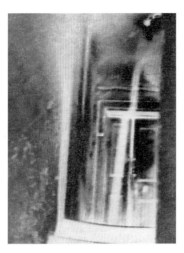

Video capture of the doorway.

Video capture of the curtain.

After pasting the scanned flower into and behind (by holding down the option key while selecting Paste Into) several areas of the image, Torinus applied the Motion Blur filter so that it appeared to be falling.

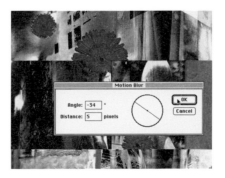

Flower with Motion Blur applied.

To add painterly effects to various parts of the image, Torinus used the Brush Strokes style of Xaos Tools's Paint Alchemy filter with the Ordered Layering option selected. Paint Alchemy lets you base the direction, size and transparency of your brushstrokes on color or brightness variations in the image, so Torinus used the Color Variations option.

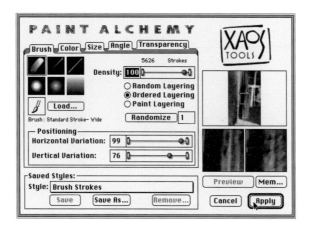

Paint Alchemy filter dialog box with Brush Strokes style selected.

After scanning the etching of the blindfolded man, Torinus inverted it to make the lines white, and then heightened the contrast to make the lines pop out more. To smooth out the video captures—the curtain and the door—she applied Photoshop's Video: De-Interlace filter (with the Interpolation option checked), which lets you eliminate either the odd or even interlaced lines in a video frame. Before pasting the video frames into square selections within the central square, she applied the Unsharp Mask filter (Filter>Sharpen) to sharpen the images. f/x

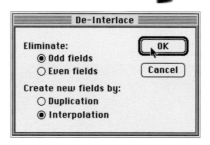

Photoshop's De-Interlace dialog box, which lets you smooth out the lines you get in video grabs.

# Section 3

# Gallery

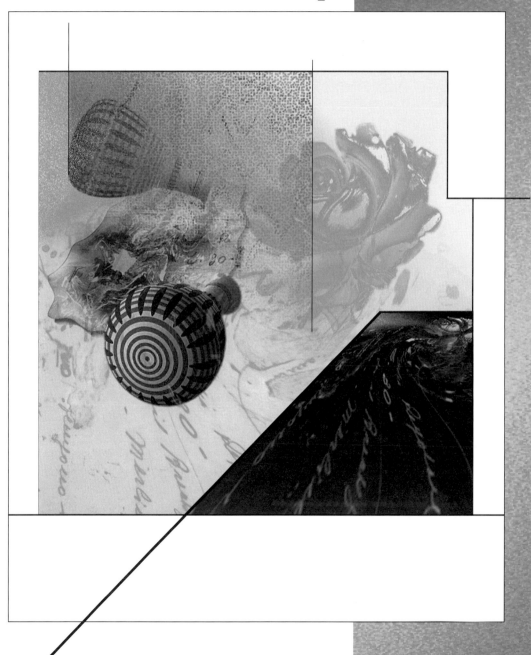

## Techniques:

This illustration for a CD cover was composited of numerous foliage shots, a boulder, a flower and a pool with the artist's own legs floating in it—all photos taken by the artist. The foliage shots were all scanned in RGB and inverted. The rock was originally scanned in grayscale, then converted to RGB and colorized using Hue/Saturation. Bradford made a selection of the boulder, so he could paste some of the foliage images behind it. To assemble the upper part of the image, he created a number of channels with gradations. Then he used another channel with a black-to-white gradation to merge the pool shot with the top part of the image. After pasting the flower on both sides of the image, he boosted the opacity as well as the saturation. Next he created the horizontal white streak, lightening it gradually in many passes using the dodge tool set to a small brush with minimal opacity. Finally, he selected the V shape with the lasso tool and inverted it.

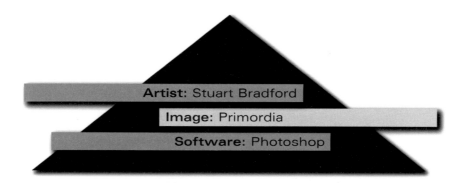

**Artist:** Stuart Bradford

**Image:** Primordia

**Software:** Photoshop

Glenn Mitsui is an artist and illustrator based in Seattle. This image was commissioned as a print ad for Ray Dream Designer to show the many different ways it can be used in conjunction with other programs like Photoshop and Painter. Mitsui began by doing a series of pencil sketches of the piece until he came up with the right composition. Then in FreeHand he did a line drawing of all the elements in the proper positions, saved it as an Illustrator 3.0 file and imported it into Photoshop to add texture and color to the background.

Next Mitsui scanned the leaves, dollar bill, Dutch stamp, map and black-and-white art. He used Indexed Color to make the map yellow and red. In Ray Dream Designer, he built wireframes of the 3D objects: the spheres, the globe, the sail, the cone and the springs. The texture maps were scanned images that he manipulated in Photoshop, saved as RGB TIFF files and imported into Ray Dream, where he mapped them onto the objects.

Finally, he brought everything back into Photoshop for compositing. As a finishing touch, he used a mask with a gradient to make the springs appear to fade out.

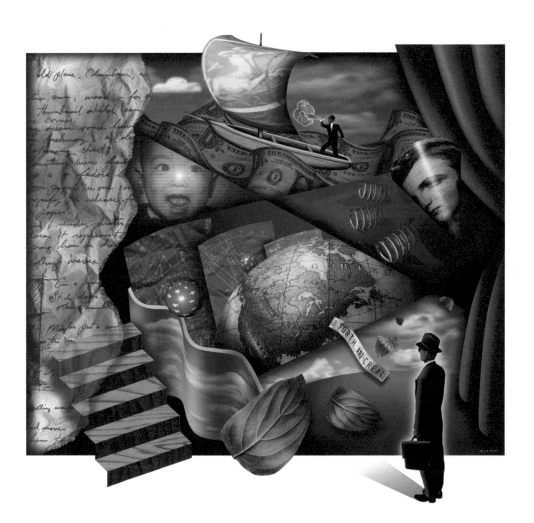

**Artist:** Glenn Mitsui

**Image:** Whole New World

**Software:** Photoshop; Fractal Design Painter; FreeHand; Ray Dream Designer

## Techniques:

For this image, Paternoster began by creating a background from a graduated fill going from light blue to lime green. She then copied and pasted rectangular selections from the background onto other areas of the background; she also used Flip vertical to reverse the direction of the gradations in these areas.

Selecting areas in the top-right section of the image, Paternoster used Photoshop's Extrude filter with the following settings: Pyramid type, Size 10, Depth 2 and Level Based. Using the Perspective command, she scaled the image to give it more depth. After copying the file and selecting irregular areas with the lasso, she used the KPT Fractal Explorer to generate a fractal pattern using the color ramp of the existing image. She copied and pasted these filtered areas in various parts of the original composition with subtle variations in opacity.

To create the rippling-water effect in the bottom-left corner, she used the Ripple filter. Using an airbrush of various colors, she painted some areas lighter and others darker.

**Artist:** Nance Paternoster

**Image:** RakuGlz

**Software:** Photoshop; Kai's Power Tools

This design piece was created for an invitation to *FAD Magazine*'s issue release party. The background of the image was created from a video grab of the inside of Torinus's computer. Because she wanted to maintain the video feel of the image, Torinus didn't use the De-Interlace filter (Filter>Video). As a result, the interlaced video lines are quite visible in some areas of the picture. To give the image more of a three-dimensional look, she distorted it with the Glass Lens Bright filter from Kai's Power Tools.

Before colorizing the black-and-white frame, she brought out its texture to give the gold reflective characteristics. After applying the Add Noise filter with an amount of 500 and Gaussian Distribution, she blurred the pixels with the Gaussian Blur filter set to a 1-pixel radius. She finished the texture with the Facet and the Emboss filters (both under Filter> Stylize). After selecting the entire texture, she pasted it inside the frame, scaling down the texture so that the frame would fit around it.

Torinus pasted the scanned flower inside the frame and copied it. She then inverted the copy, changed the hue and pasted the copy into the selection of the frame.

Torinus created the text in Pixar Typestry, saving each letter to a different channel in the Photoshop file until she had adjusted all the colors in relation to each other.

To give the image more depth, she saved two alpha channels for creating shadows, one on the left side of the frame, and one underneath. In both channels she used the gradient tool to draw a gradation. After loading each channel, she used the Brightness/Contrast command to darken the areas that were farther away to create depth of field.

**Artist:** Sigi Torinus

**Image:** Life

**Software:** Photoshop; Kai's Power Tools

Bradford scanned some crumpled tissue paper in grayscale (a favorite technique of his) to create the background texture, which he colorized red and then cut and pasted until it resembled fabric. To create the uneven edges around the texture area, he made a path with the pen tool, made the path into a selection and saved it to a channel. He then loaded the selection, selected the inverse and deleted the rest of the texture. Using this texture as the background, Bradford then added a new layer. After opening another file—a scanned photo he took of some lawn chairs—he roughly selected the area he wanted with the lasso tool. He then copied that selection and pasted it onto the new layer. Then he set the Layer Options to Lighten mode and about 20 percent opacity and added a layer mask. With the blend tool, he created a gradation in the layer mask, which was used to fade the image of the lawn chairs and merge it into the textural background. After using the same process to add the church steeple image, he flattened the layers.

The small photograph was another of the artist's photos. He scanned it in RGB, copied it, pasted it into the image and saved the selection to a channel before deselecting it.

The type was scanned from an old postcard and saved to another channel; there he applied the Wave filter to get a subtle, flowing effect. Next he inverted the type channel, loaded it and filled it with black to make the type black. He then reloaded the channel for the inset photo and inverted that, which made the figure ghost-like and the type white.

**Artist:** Stuart Bradford

**Image:** Her Singing Mind

**Software:** Photoshop

## Techniques:

This image depicts Famine, one of the four horsemen of the Apocalypse. Krause used the Brightness/Contrast command to saturate the reds and yellows and lighten the image. In the Channels palette, she duplicated the black channel of the child image by dragging the black channel onto the new channel icon at the bottom of the palette. In the Curves dialog box, she increased the contrast of the channel by drawing with the pencil tool across the bottom edge of the grid from the left edge to the center and across the top from the right to the center. After removing the background with a white airbrush, Krause duplicated the high-contrast channel as a selection. Before returning to the CMYK channel, she copied the selection and pasted it into the image of the horseman using Darken mode at 100 percent opacity. She dragged the copy of the black channel onto the new selection icon at the bottom of the Channels palette to create her selection. Then she copied this selection and pasted the layer (Edit>Paste Layer) in Darken mode.

**Artist:** Dorothy Simpson Krause

**Image:** Horseman of the Apocalypse

**Software:** Photoshop

## Techniques:

Dorothy Krause is a fine artist who lives in Marshfield Hills, Massachusetts. For this fine art piece, Krause combined the child's face and a crystal ball topped with a gold head of Hathor from the Boston Museum of Fine Art's Nubian Collection. To create the glowing, negative quality of the face, she copied and pasted the face onto a new layer and used the freehand option in the Curves dialog box to dramatically alter the colors. In Layer Options she applied the Luminosity mode and set the opacity at 50 percent. She added the crystal ball by pasting it on another layer and positioning it over the child's face, using Layer Options to specify Darken mode. To bring in the highlights, she pasted a copy of the crystal ball onto another layer in Lighten mode. Using the rubber stamp tool, she cloned parts of both original images to intensify those areas in the composited image and bring them up to 100 percent opacity. The gold areas were enhanced with the Metallic/Gentle Gold filter in KTP's Gradient Designer.

Artist: Dorothy Simpson Krause

Image: Child of Nubia

Software: Photoshop; Kai's Power Tools

235

Gallery

## Techniques:

This image, like many of Manske's images, began with a traditional collage that he scanned into Photoshop. Using the lasso to select certain areas, he applied filters and adjusted the contrast and color levels. After posterizing the image to about 8 levels, he changed the mode from RGB to Indexed Color, which—because it drastically reduces the number of colors used in the image—shrank the file size from 12mb to 2mb. Manske uses Indexed Color for most of his images because he prefers the traditional block- or screen-printed feel it gives to his work, compared to the smooth continuous-tone look you get with millions of colors.

Because Manske rarely uses more than 50 colors in an image, he finds it unnecessary to convert his final images to RGB mode. However, they must be converted to RGB if you plan to use filters or layers, neither will work in Indexed Color mode.

To select the areas in the image to be colorized, he used the magic wand with Tolerance set to 1 and the Anti-aliased option unchecked to click on an area of a particular color. Then he chose Similar from the Select menu to select all the areas containing that color and filled them with a new color from his customized palette. To fill other areas, he used the Paintbrush with stylus pressure set to Size. (*Note:* This option is available only if you use a pressure-sensitive tablet.)

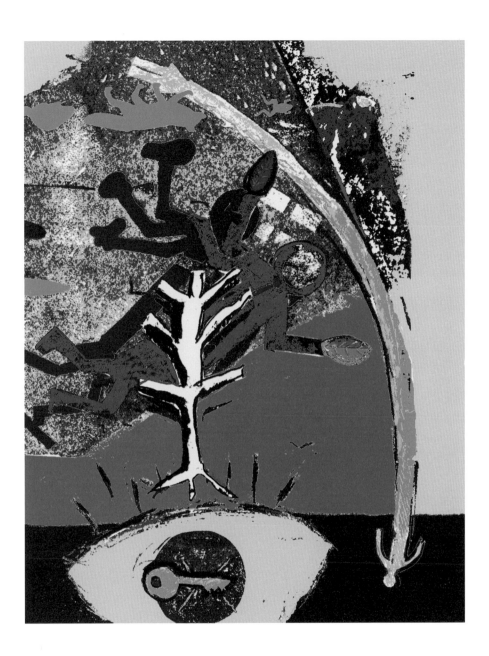

Artist: Kent Manske

Image: Sense Dance

Software: Photoshop

## Techniques:

**H**elen Golden is a Palo Alto, California-based photographer and digital artist. Golden used her own etching as the basis of this image, which she scanned into Photoshop. After colorizing the image with Curves, Golden increased the canvas size. Then, to make it look like a reflection, she selected the image, copied it and flipped it upside down, inverted it, and pasted the whole image onto a new layer at 60 percent opacity in Normal mode. To simulate a double reflection, she pasted it again at the same settings. Golden selected the entire image, inverted it, then pasted it onto a new layer at 80 percent opacity in Lighten mode, which gave the central part of the image a scratchy texture. With the water at the bottom selected, she used Color Balance to make it blue. To fine-tune the colors, she adjusted Levels, then used the clone tool to clean up various areas. To make the reflection of the trees look a little different than the originals, not quite a mirror image, she used the clone tool on different parts of the trees at different opacity levels.

**Artist:** Helen S. Golden

**Image:** Ancient Landscape

**Software:** Photoshop

For this fine art piece, Wylde combined the traditional print media of relief printing and lithography with digital tools. The multicolored background was created from a relief print that she scanned in color at 144 dpi, the facial profile from an original lithograph scanned as line art. Because Wylde wanted the profile to fit into the image of the ear, she changed its image size so that it matched the size of the ear. To combine the two images, she pasted the profile onto a layer and then adjusted the mode to Normal and opacity to 95 percent in the Layer Options. After widening the canvas size enough to accommodate the left panel, she pasted that into the illustration and then pasted the scanned hands over it. Using the selection marquee, Wylde selected a four-pixel-wide area where the panel met the background texture and applied the Blur filter to soften the edge between them. To smooth out the jaggies in the pixelated hands, she selected the entire left panel and alternately applied the Blur and Sharpen More filters several times.

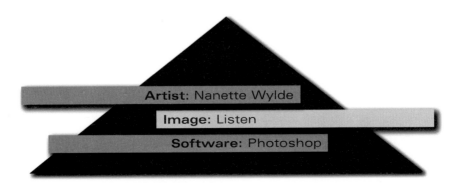

**Artist:** Nanette Wylde

**Image:** Listen

**Software:** Photoshop

## Techniques:

This art piece was composited from three images—all photos shot by the artist. The one on the left was a photo of a hand holding a flower scanned in RGB and inverted. The two overlapping images of the closeup face and the woman hanging upside down were actually a single sequence from a television program the artist shot with a 35mm camera at just the right moment as one faded into the other. After scanning the image in grayscale, Bradford converted it to Duotone mode. The ear was another grayscale scan that he converted to RGB, colorized and then inverted. To simulate a rough, torn-paper effect, he cropped the ear using the lasso tool and a Wacom tablet. The narrow tone that cuts through the center of the image he also selected with the lasso tool and then boosted its saturation. The eye color was altered using the Colorize option in Hue/Saturation.

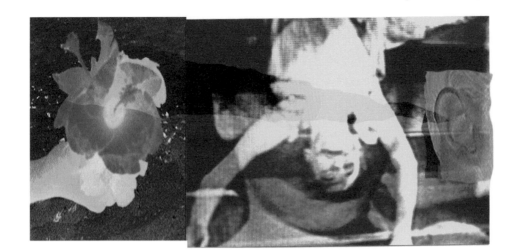

**Artist:** Stuart Bradford

**Image:** Language Means Nothing

**Software:** Photoshop

## Techniques:

The artist began this image in Painter, painting the background and the sunflower in the left corner. The figure was drawn with a combination of the pen, chalk and airbrush tools. After applying a cottonlike paper texture to the surface, she used the airbrush to give some of the shapes (the sunflower and the jacket buttons) a 3D appearance. After importing the image into Photoshop, she used KPT's Glass Lens Bright filter to spherize the 3D eyes and head. Next she inverted the map (Image>Map), scaled down the head and pasted it into the background. Bringing the image back into Painter, Paternoster copied the face, made it a floating selection in PainterX2 and varied the brightness/contrast/opacity. Next she applied the Glass Distortion option (Effects>Focus) to the face. Finally, she applied lighting (Effects> Surface Control>Apply Lighting) using the "dumb lites" setting with an extra light positioned to accent certain parts of the composition.

**Artist:** Nance Paternoster

**Image:** Mr.ButLadee

**Software:** Photoshop; Fractal Design Painter; PainterX2; Kai's Power Tools

## Techniques:

*Dream Space* was created by scanning (with Ofoto) a scrap of crumpled acrylic painted canvas from one of the artist's original paintings. Lhotka uses LightSource's scanning software Ofoto because it lets her save the colors from her acrylic paintings as her digital palette. From this, she created both her color palette and the starting point for the image. Next, she brought the image into Painter and added the river that runs through the image by cutting it out as a frisket. She filled it with a blend and applied the Watercolor Rough paper texture. After bringing it back into Photoshop, she repeatedly cut, copied and rotated pieces of the scanned canvas to assemble the composition. Colors were repeatedly changed using Photoshop's Hue/Saturation command; she increased saturation to +10; for every copied and pasted selection, she changed the hue to constantly shift the color palette. Lhotka made a duplicate of the image, saved that to a new file, and cut out large rectangular areas and pasted them individually onto the original file. Finally, she increased the contrast to 15; this was done to compensate for the enlarging of the image for printing to an Iris printer.

**Artist:** Bonny Lhotka

**Image:** Dream Space

**Software:** Photoshop; Fractal Design Painter; Ofoto

## Techniques:

This image began with a photograph of a rock texture, a black-and-white photo of a mannequin and a black-and-white photo of a paper bird model. The fern leaves were scanned directly.

After opening the mannequin, Miller used Hue/Saturation to colorize it a brownish tan so it would blend in with the colors in the rock texture. She used the path tool to select the mannequin and copied that, then placed it on a new layer on top of the rock texture. She wanted the mannequin to look like a fossil, so she used Layer Options to adjust the underlying and floating selections—as well as setting the opacity to 45 percent—until the rock texture showed through. She used Color Balance to accentuate the reds in the mannequin's face. To make the face pop out even more, she put a copy of the original face on a new layer over the manipulated one at about 15 percent opacity.

The white profile was a scan of an old engraving; Miller used the magic wand tool to select the black lines; after all the lines were selected, she made the lines into a path and saved the path. Although she experimented by filling the path with different colors, she eventually decided that white lines worked best. But the original lines weren't thick enough, so she selected the path and stroked it with 2 pixels of white to add thickness without changing the contours. Because she felt the image needed something more, she cut out the image of the bird. To achieve a sepia-tone color, she changed it from grayscale to RGB mode, then used Hue/Saturation to add color. She used the gradient tool in Multiply mode and applied it to many different selections of the bird to create the many subtle gradations in its wings and body.

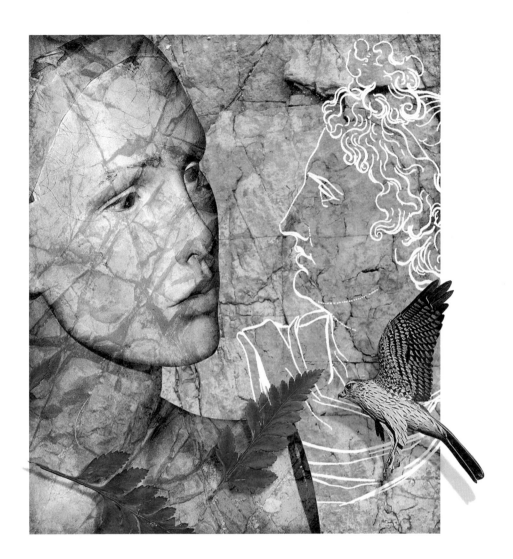

**Artist:** Judy L. Miller

**Image:** Past/Present

**Software:** Photoshop

249

Gallery

## Techniques:

For this fine art piece, Lhotka wove strips of canvas from one of her acrylic paintings into a checkerboard pattern, which she then scanned using Ofoto scanning software, so she could match her original acrylic colors. After opening the file in Photoshop, she increased Contrast to 15 and then applied the Sharpen filter to make the image crisp. Then she used the lasso tool to cut out some of the woven areas and used the gradient tool to create the sky. Various areas were reworked using several Photoshop tools: the pen, the paintbrush and the smudge tool. She increased Saturation to +15 to make the colors more dense for printing to a large format (18 by 16 inches).

**Artist:** Bonny Lhotka

**Image:** High Country

**Software:** Photoshop; Ofoto

251

This image began with two black-and-white photos: the photo on the left Golden took of someone walking past an office window. After scanning it, instead of putting the image at right angles on the canvas, she rotated it a few degrees to give it a more dynamic feeling so the converging lines would look slightly off balance. In Curves she tried different settings to punch up the colors and generate a mood of stark drama. Then she fine-tuned the colors in Color Balance and Hue/Saturation to increase the contrast. She applied the Find Edges filter but because the result was too sharp, she had to use the smudge tool to soften some of the edges of the figure. After copying the left side of the image, she scaled it down a little and pasted it over the original image on a new layer in Darken mode. Then she used the clone tool with the Non-aligned option to cover areas of the double image that were too busy.

The other photo of the figure on the right the artist printed in the darkroom using a technique that made it resemble a negative. Once it was scanned, she inverted it to make it a positive. After removing all the background until only the woman remained, she selected it using the lasso with an 8-pixel feather. Then she pasted it over the Venetian blinds on a new layer at about 35 percent opacity in Normal mode. Using the dodge/burn/sponge tool, she lightened and darkened selective areas of the image, using dodge to make it appear as if the blinds were going through the pole on the right.

**Artist:** Helen S. Golden

**Image:** The Direction Is Arbitrary

**Software:** Photoshop

## Techniques:

Adigard did this editorial illustration about a rock band for *Ray Gun* magazine. He modeled the 3D cylinders in Ray Dream Designer, then created the texture map of hands in Photoshop from two different scans of his own hands. Adigard frequently scans objects directly, rather than using photographs of them. The surface texture in the background was no exception; it originated from a bag made of chain links that Adigard found at a flea market in France. After scanning it into Photoshop, he pasted it into another layer and then chose Lighten mode from the Layers palette. The center image was another scanned object: a small bottle covered with sequins; he then cut out the shape he wanted in Photoshop.

**Artist:** Erik Adigard, M.A.D.

**Image:** Grace

**Software:** Photoshop; Ray Dream Designer

Jasin began by scanning a photo he'd taken of a marble wall. To punch up the marble's colors, he used Color Balance, Curves, Levels and Hue/ Saturation. To create a spiral, he applied the Polar Coordinates filter with the Rectangular to Polar setting, smoothing away the center seam with the rubber stamp tool.

Jasin then created another layer and filled it with black. In a layer mask, he created a radial gradation (with white in the center and black at the edges) over the spiral. In the black areas of the mask, all the colors showed through; in the white areas, the black layer showed through; while a combination of the two showed through the gray areas in varying degrees. The effect was the illusion of a 3D sphere.

To create the small sphere on the right, Jasin copied a circular selection of the middle sphere and pasted it to a new layer. After scaling it down, he applied the KPT Spherize filter and then Photoshop's Zigzag filter set to 5 ridges, with the "Out from Center" option selected.

For the large spiral on the left, he copied the middle sphere and reduced the resolution. To limit the color palette, he switched to Indexed Color and chose 6 bits-per-pixel resolution, Diffusion dither and Adaptive palette. Back in RGB—and before boosting the resolution back up—he changed the interpolation method to Nearest Neighbor. This allowed him to preserve the square pixels, since he upped the resolution in even increments by twice doubling the size of the file to 400 percent. He resized it up again, making sure to reinterpolate it evenly as before. Finally, he pasted it onto a new layer, moving the left triangle on the Floating slider slightly to the right to drop out the black pixels in the spiral so some of the background would show through.

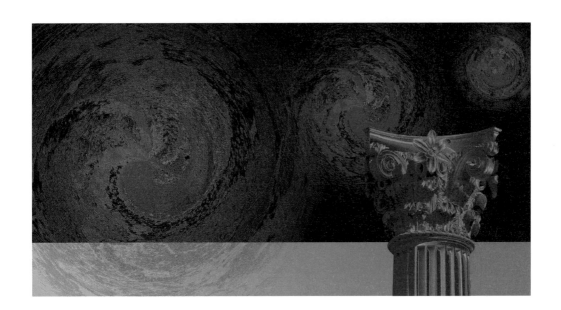

**Artist:** Mark Jasin

**Image:** Three Spheres

**Software:** Photoshop; Kai's Power Tools

## Techniques:

This illustration was done for an article in *Vogue* magazine about the future of fashion. The dress, the hat and the cables were modeled in Ray Dream Designer. The background was a combination of three different images, one originated in Illustrator, and two in Ray Dream. Adigard then brought the background into Photoshop, where he manipulated each image individually, colorizing them with Hue/ Saturation and applying Gaussian Blur to one of the images. To simulate a fabric texture, he pasted each image on a separate layer and used Layer Options to set different modes and opacities.

To create the blurry texture on the boots, he applied the Wave filter to them, then applied Motion Blur separately to four different sections of the boots and blended them into the legs with the smudge tool.

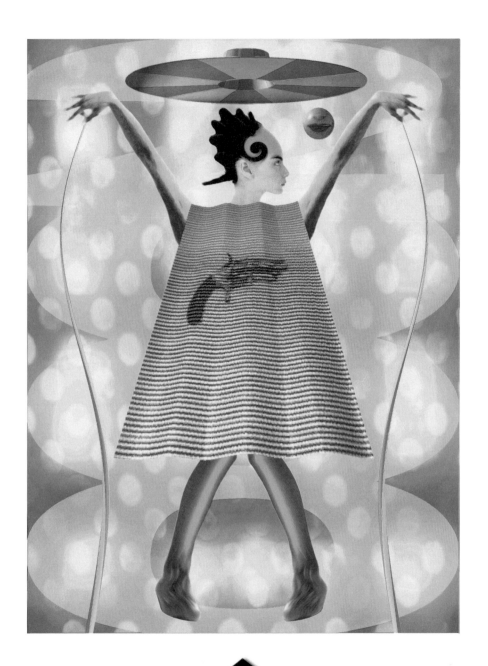

**Artist:** Erik Adigard, M.A.D.

**Image:** Vogue 2000

**Software:** Photoshop; Illustrator; Ray Dream Designer

## Techniques:

Lund photographed the flag with a Leaf Digital Camera. In Photoshop he duplicated the image and applied Photoshop's Extrude filter (Filter>Stylize>Extrude) to the duplicate. In the filter's dialog box, he changed the 3D object default (type) setting from Blocks to Pyramids, set both Size and Depth to 20 and left the random button selected. In the Brightness/Contrast dialog box, he boosted the Contrast to +30. After pasting the extruded duplicate on a new layer over the original flag, he double-clicked on the layer to bring up the Layer Options dialog box. There, he moved the Underlying slider (white triangle) to the left—a setting of 198— until the image had the deteriorated look he was after. Finally, after flattening the layers, he applied Gallery Effects's Craquelure filter, with Crack Spacing set to 31, Crack Depth to 10 and Crack Brightness to 7.

**Artist:** John Lund, Photodigital

**Image:** Cracked Flag

**Software:** Photoshop; Gallery Effects

This image appeared on the cover of the *Photoshop Handbook 2.5 Edition,* by David Beidney, Bert Monroy and Mark Siprut, published by Random House. It's one thing to scan in bottles and stuffed hearts, but a delicate flower? Adigard accomplished this feat by tying the rose to a string and suspending it just above the scanner.

Once the rose was safely preserved in Photoshop, he selected the shadowy areas between the petals and inverted them to make them white. Because midtones were also picked up in addition to the dark shadows, and they turned from red to blue when inverted, he had to move the Hue/Saturation slider from one side to the other to change the hue back to red. Using Composite Controls, he composited three different versions of the rose—the original scan, a high-contrast, blurred version and an inverted version—to control the amount of sharpness and blur in the final image. (*Note:* In Photoshop 3.0 he would have pasted each rose on a different layer and then adjusted the opacity of each layer in the Layers palette.)

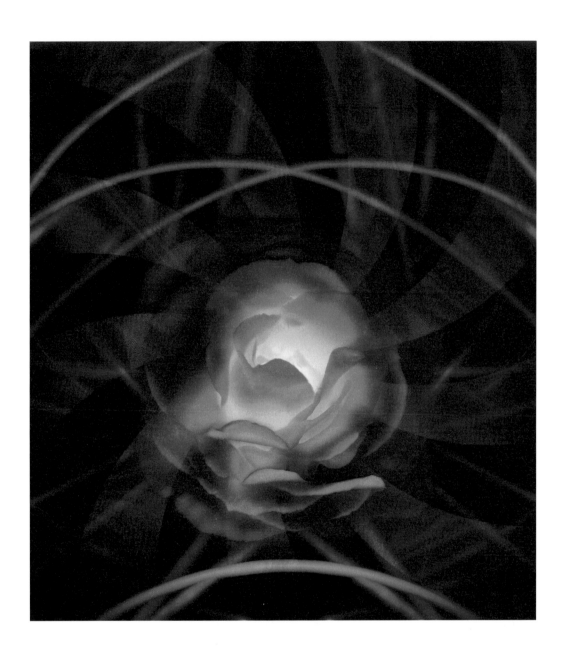

**Artist:** Erik Adigard, M.A.D.

**Image:** Rose

**Software:** Photoshop

## Techniques:

After scanning in a rough sketch, Corinne Okada, a San Francisco artist and illustrator, cleaned up the lines in Photoshop by upping the contrast. After lassoing areas with a 60-pixel feather, she filled them in Darken mode with a flat shade of purple to add color without obscuring the pencil lines. Using the dodge/burn/sponge tool, she set Exposure to 50 percent and alternated between the shadow areas, midtones and highlights to give depth and definition to the woman. This tool allowed her to shade the figure more quickly than she could have with the airbrush because she could darken the image without having to switch colors in the palette. Even more important, using the dodge/burn/sponge tool (with both fine and large feathered brushes) let her bring subtle expressions to the face that would be difficult to achieve with any other tool. Finally, in PainterX2, she used the charcoal and airbrush to add texture, color and the suggestion of a shoji screen.

**Artist:** Corinne Okada

**Image:** Crane Maiden

**Software:** Photoshop; Fractal Design Painter; PainterX2

265

## Techniques:

This image was originally commissioned by *Publish* magazine, but was never used. The background is a photograph of water that was rescaled to alter its proportions. Bradford created the arch with the pen tool, then made it into a selection. After inverting the selection, he adjusted Levels to darken the outer edge. The oval shape at the bottom was merely a small section of the background inverted. The figure came from a television image Bradford shot with a 35mm camera that he scanned in grayscale and converted to a duotone. The shadow to the right of the figure was a path drawn with the pen tool, converted to a selection and colorized with Hue/Saturation. The type and arched line were created in Illustrator and imported, then copied and pasted one at a time into separate channels in Photoshop and loaded and filled with color. After selecting the fire, Bradford altered it with the Distort command (Image>Effects>Distort) until he got the shape he wanted, then he pasted it behind the letter A. To soften the transition between the fire and the background, he blurred the edges of the fire by zooming in so he could edit them pixel by pixel. The halo of type at the top was done in Illustrator, pasted into a channel in Photoshop, loaded and filled with color. The vertical handwritten type was scanned, then scaled and distorted in a channel, which was loaded and filled with white.

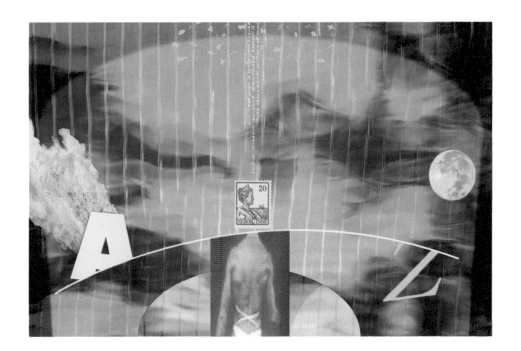

**Artist:** Stuart Bradford

**Image:** Constant Baptism

**Software:** Photoshop; Illustrator

This image, meant to represent the human spirit's dualistic nature, was created from black-and-white infrared photographs, a photo and an etching. Soshea scanned the original black-and-white infrared image of the mythological god Apollo into Photoshop. Using Hue/Saturation, he colorized the image red, then saved it as a separate RGB file. After boosting the contrast of the original scan, he inverted it into a negative black-and-white image, which he then copied and pasted into an alpha channel in the colorized Apollo file. Scanning a Polaroid of the devil mask at the approximate size of Apollo's head, Soshea colorized it purple and deleted the background so that only the devil image was visible. He outlined the devil image by selecting the black outside area of the mask with the magic wand, then inverting the selection and copying it to the Clipboard. After loading the channel of the red Apollo image, he pasted the devil mask into the shadow area of Apollo. To merge the two images, he used the smudge tool and the Blur and Add Noise filters. The effect of Apollo's hair coming over the top of the devil's head was a fortunate coincidence. Soshea scanned an etching of a skull and inverted it to produce white lines on a black field. Then he copied and pasted it into another channel. Through a series of minute scaling adjustments and repositioning of the skull's active alpha selection (Command-option), he aligned the skull channel with the facial structure. The skull image was then imprinted into the face through Fill/Darken in the Edit menu. Finally, he scanned in a black-and-white infrared photo of a sunset, then colorized and pasted it into a slightly feathered background area of the Apollo Diablo image.

Artist: Steven Soshea

Image: Apollo Diablo

Software: Photoshop

269

## Techniques:

Created as a design for a T-shirt, this image originated from one of M.A.D.'s seemingly inexhaustible supply of unusual objects: a rubber finger-puppet clown. After scanning the clown, McShane selected areas using the lasso with a large feather and used Color Balance on those areas to alter the colors. The spiral was hand-drawn with a pencil, then photocopied. To degenerate the original image, she enlarged the copy and photocopied it again, repeating the process several times; the idea was to break up the black areas so the white lines would show through. Finally, she pasted the deteriorated spiral onto a separate layer over the clown image, inverted it and set the mode to Lighten so that only the white areas of the spiral showed through.

**Artist:** Patricia McShane, M.A.D.

**Image:** Spiral Clown

**Software:** Photoshop

## Techniques:

To create this illustration for *Ray Gun* magazine, McShane scanned a hand-written letter
and colorized it with a linear blend from green
to yellow by pasting the gradation on a new
layer in Darken mode so that it was superim-
posed over the letter. Next, she pasted in a scan
of a puppet head. After pasting the scan again
on top of the first scan, she applied the Motion
Blur filter set to 6 pixels. She set the Layer
Options to Lighten mode, which produced an
unusual effect—making the puppet's face look
as if it was wrapped in cellophane—and let only
the blurred highlights show through. To create
the globular pattern, she took an image of
extremely large monochrome dots scanned from
a fragment of a discarded billboard and pasted
it onto a new layer in Color mode.

**Artist:** Patricia McShane, M.A.D.

**Image:** Come Play with Me

**Software:** Photoshop

273

*Gallery*

Peters, an artist and illustrator who specializes in collages, used a combination of elements for this image. The car interior was from an old *National Geographic;* the pattern in the dashboard was the result of large halftone dots from the original photo; the map was taken from a road atlas. The TV was from a magazine ad; Peters distorted it with Perspective and used Distort to pull out the top-right corner. The planet was a foam ball designed to look like earth; the object was scanned directly and the colors changed with Hue/Saturation. The eye was a scanned photo that he pasted into the TV screen and distorted with Perspective to completely fill the screen. The falling object is a couch; he duplicated it and pasted the copy behind the original. Applying the Motion Blur filter to the duplicate (angle set to 90° and distance at 50 pixels) produced a blurred image in back while the one in front was still sharp, making the couch appear to be hurtling downward. To create the bullseye, Peters made a series of concentric rings using the elliptical marquee. After making a selection with the marquee, he used the Command key to deselect an interior portion of the selected circle, leaving an outer ring selected. He copied and pasted it over the original and filled it with red, then adjusted opacity to 40 percent, repeating the same process for the other rings. To create the shadow of the TV set, Peters selected a rectangular area with the lasso while holding down the option key to get a straight line. Using the gradient tool with 40 percent opacity in Darken mode, he made a blend from the TV to the left to create the shadow effect. To alter the word Aurora, he used Perspective to squeeze the left side and Distort to pull out the right side.

**Artist:** David Peters

**Image:** Wayne's World

**Software:** Photoshop

This image was done for *Network Computing*, a monthly magazine, to illustrate a story on navigating the Internet. To create the floor, Peters made a selection with the elliptical marquee and pasted it under the desk. After using the Perspective and Distort commands to get the shape he wanted, he applied a graduated fill. But he wanted a more textured effect, so he applied Gallery Effects's Craquelure filter with a crack depth of 7, crack spacing about 20 and a brightness value of 9. Next he applied Gallery Effects's Emboss filter with Light Position set to bottom left and a Relief value of 13; inverting the image produced the white lines. He then selected background area underneath the desk, copied and pasted it behind the circular floor.

To make the angle of the floor match that of the desk, Peters used Perspective to compress the circle and Distort to pull out the left side of the floor; then he copied and pasted it again behind itself. To create the drop shadow, he moved the floor slightly down and to the right and filled it with a green blend.

The three tubular openings in the desk were created with the Large Metallic Cylinder setting of KPT's Gradient Designer filter. To create the effect of flowing letters, Peters used various combinations of Perspective, Distort, Rotate and Opacity. The wood texture came from a scanned photo of a wooden fence; the Hue/Saturation command gave the side of the desk a yellowish and greenish look. For the desktop, he selected a section of the original scan and scaled it up to accentuate the grain, then used Hue/Saturation again to give it a washed, stained look and a lavender hue.

**Artist:** David Peters

**Image:** The Internet Deamon

**Software:** Photoshop; Gallery Effects; Kai's Power Tools

Lund began by scanning a photo of water; from that he made a circular selection and feathered it 64 pixels. He first applied the Twirl filter at a 50° angle and then Radial Blur using the Spin blur method, with Amount set to 21 and the Quality option set to good. After darkening the image to -80 in the Brightness/Contrast dialog box, he made another much smaller circular selection in the center of the twirled water, feathered it 20 pixels, darkened it again by moving the Brightness slider all the way to the left and increased Contrast to +30.

The image of the earth was a NASA shot, which he scaled down, then copied and pasted into the water image. Using the lasso tool with a 25-pixel feather radius, he deselected a portion of the earth to make it appear as if it was submerged in the water. After reselecting the earth with the pen tool, he deselected the upper-left two-thirds of the earth with the lasso using a 30-pixel feather. This left a crescent-shaped selection at the lower-right edge of the earth that gradated from a hard edge at the lower right to a soft feathered edge at the upper left. To give the earth a rounder look, he darkened it by setting Brightness to -40. Using the lasso with an 8-pixel feather, he selected a small section of the water just below and to the right of the earth and reduced Brightness to -40, which made the earth appear to be casting a shadow on the water.

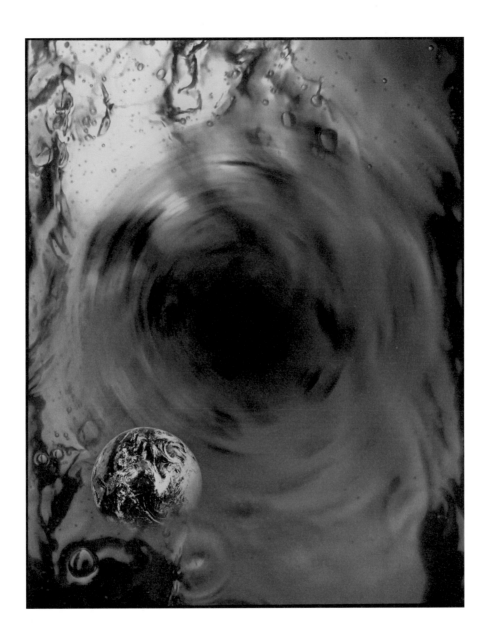

**Artist:** John Lund, Photodigital

**Image:** Down the Drain

**Software:** Photoshop

## Techniques:

This image was a fun, self-promotion piece. Peters took an old postcard and some scrap photos from which various elements had been previously cut out, leaving silhouettes of the images. One was a photo of a rubber chicken against a blue sky with the chicken cut out; another was a photo of a coil spring from an old truck with a piece of rebar running through it. Because he'd cut the rubber chicken out at an angle, it left a visible edge on the remaining part of the photo, which was even more apparent after he scanned it.

He used his three-pass scanner as an image-manipulation tool. He put the coil spring scan underneath the chicken scan so that the coil silhouette showed through the chicken silhouette. Because the coils were cut out, the background from a scanned texture he'd placed underneath showed through as well. For each of the three passes, he moved the composited scans in different directions during the scanning process, which added some colors to areas of the scan.

Then Peters placed a scanned photo of a diver with the diver cut on top of another photo of water so that the water showed through the silhouette of the cutout diver; using the lasso tool to select the outline of the diver, he saved that as a separate element in a different file—producing a diver filled with water; he then pasted that into the illustration.

To create some unusual effects with the postcard, he scanned it three times in three different ways: the first time as a regular scan; the second time he moved it to the right edge of the scanner and scanned it for two of the scanner's three passes, then moved it to the left side for the third pass; just as with the other composited scans, letting in light changed the colors.

**Artist:** David Peters

**Image:** Greetings from So. California

**Software:** Photoshop

# Techniques:

Judy Miller is a photo-illustrator based in Tucson, Arizona. The centerpiece of this image is a photo the artist herself had taken of an agave plant—a black-and-white print that she hand-colored with oil paint and colored pencils. After scanning the photo into Photoshop, Miller used the pen tool to cut slices of the plant, which she pasted one by one into a new file. There she applied various filters to different slices, such as the Wind filter, the Facet filter, Unsharp Mask, Sharpen, Sharpen More, Sharpen Edges. She also did color adjustments with Color Balance on individual sections and the entire image.

Once the image was composited, she adjusted Curves to accentuate the reds in some of the shadow areas. To create all but the bottom part of the border, she selected a small area of one of the leaves for its color and texture and chose the Define Pattern command (Edit menu). With the pen tool, she selected the area where she wanted to place the pattern—in this case, the top, left and right borders—and filled the area (using the Fill command in the Edit menu) with the pattern, which tiled the small section over and over. To add the inside dark border, she repeated the process with a darker section of the image. For the bottom edge, she selected an area of the gravel (which she also defined as a pattern) and tiled that.

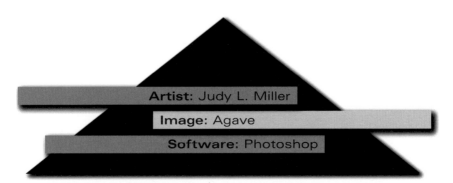

**Artist:** Judy L. Miller

**Image:** Agave

**Software:** Photoshop

## Techniques:

Helen Golden, a Palo Alto, California-based photographer and digital artist, began this image by scanning in an out-of-focus grainy photo of four dancing figures. After boosting the contrast in Brightness/Contrast, she selected the four figures and copied, pasted and inverted them—then increased the contrast again until not much was left but their outlines. In the Effects submenu in the Image menu, she used Scale, Distort and Skew to push and pull the outlines until she got the effect she was after. With the outlines still selected, Golden applied the Blur filter repeatedly and copied the blurred outline. Inverting the outline to darken it, she feathered the edge, then used Distort again. The feathering created a white ghostlike ragged line around the black line. After selecting the black-and-white outline, she inverted it, pasting the new outline into the area underneath the three figures in the center of the image. For the finishing touches, she used the smudge and dodge/burn/sponge tools.

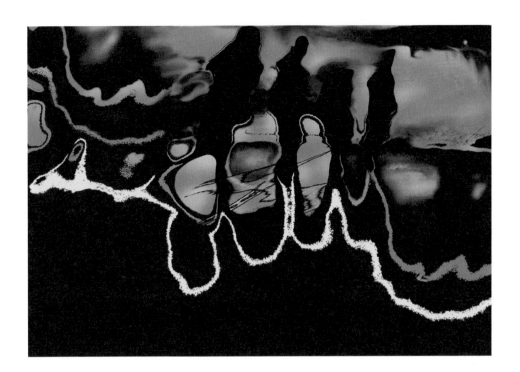

**Artist:** Helen S. Golden

**Image:** Ancestors

**Software:** Photoshop

## Techniques:

The artichoke image began as a pencil drawing that Wylde scanned in at 16 levels of gray at 144 dpi. After opening the image in Photoshop, she switched to RGB mode. In the Color Balance dialog box, she set Color Levels for Midtones to -34 (Cyan/Red), +56 (Magenta/ Green) and +30 (Yellow/Blue); she set Shadows to -24, +21 and +30. Next she applied the Blur filter to soften the image. With a brush set at 20 percent opacity, she painted lavender highlights. After painting the silhouetted figure in a separate document, Wylde copied and pasted it onto the artichoke, then softened the edges of the figure with the waterdrop.

**Artist:** Nanette Wylde

**Image:** Howl Asylum

**Software:** Photoshop

## Techniques:

This image was one of a series of four prints Peters did for an art exhibit in Los Angeles called "Brad Benedict's Sideshow #4." Peters began by creating the background layer and added the various elements on separate layers. The mountains and cave dwellings came from a scanned photo; after pasting the original on the left side, he copied the scan, flopped it and pasted it on the right side; then he added more cave dwellings to that side to minimize the carbon copy effect. To simulate depth and perspective, he cut and pasted smaller versions of the cave dwellings onto three different layers—each in Normal mode at 80 percent opacity—and placed them behind the original mountains layer. Then he used Image>Effects>Scale on two of the new layers to slightly alter the shape of some of the cave dwellings.

He built the screaming woman in a separate file, which consisted of four separate layers; the first was an oval background. The second was the purple border, which he created by making a layer in a solid color; using the elliptical marquee, he selected the inside oval and deleted it. Next, he scanned the woman's face onto a third layer and distorted it with the Perspective and Skew commands. The fourth layer was the green background; Peters selected the area behind the face, gave it a gradient fill and saved it as a separate layer.

The astronaut—a scanned image from a lenticular art postcard (commonly known as winky art)—was pasted on a layer in Luminosity mode at 60 percent opacity and posterized to 10 levels to give it a ghostlike effect. The Saturn image was pasted on another layer at 32 percent opacity in Normal mode.

**Artist:** David Peters

**Image:** Mystery Meat

**Software:** Photoshop

## Techniques:

Corinne Okada is a San Francisco artist and illustrator. She began this piece by scanning in a rough pencil sketch. In Photoshop, she boosted the contrast to eliminate stray pencil lines. After selecting broad areas with the lasso tool set to a 60-pixel feather, she used the Fill command in Darken mode to apply flat colors without obscuring the pencil lines. In PainterX2, Okada darkened and refined the lines and added a charcoal texture.

To create the pattern on the yoke of the girl's dress, she applied Terrazzo to a small section of a cotton rice bag she'd scanned into Photoshop. In Terrazzo, she tiled the pattern and saved it in TIFF format so she could open it in Painter. After selecting the entire image in Painter, Okada used the Capture Texture command to turn the pattern into a new paper texture, which then appeared in the Paper Palette window. With the new paper texture selected, she applied the fabric with a variety of tools, including watercolor and charcoal. She finished the image in Photoshop by bumping up the contrast again.

**Artist:** Corinne Okada

**Image:** New Muumuu

**Software:** Photoshop; Fractal Design Painter; PainterX2

## Techniques:

This image was created for one of a series of greeting cards done for Pillow Talk, a card publisher. Adigard began by creating a background composited from different photos of flames; he then applied the Wave filter to the composite. The spiral was a 3D object that Adigard modeled in Ray Dream Designer; he then mapped a wood texture onto it. After importing it into Photoshop, he used Color Balance to change the colors on the wood. The heart was another object Adigard happened to have in the studio: a small velvet pillow that was framed with gold tinsel; he scanned it and feathered it in Photoshop.

**Artist:** Erik Adigard, M.A.D.

**Image:** Ignite

**Software:** Photoshop; Ray Dream Designer

293

After scanning in a rough sketch of a wood-block print of a butterfly, Okada opened the image in Illustrator as a template and redrew it as a PostScript object. Next, she scanned a sheet of rice paper into Photoshop, where she colorized it by selecting all and filling it with a shade of purple in Darken mode. To give the rice paper a more subtle texture, she selected all and inverted the image. To composite the rice paper background with the butterfly print, she put them both onto different layers and set the Layer Options to Multiply mode. After merging the layers, Okada brought the composited image into Painter, where she added paper-texture fragments to the butterflies and the sky. Finally, she brought the image back into Photoshop to add accent color. To keep the color from spilling over the woodcut's black lines, she used a medium brush in Darken mode.

**Artist:** Corinne Okada

**Image:** Butterfly and Rice Paper

**Software:** Photoshop; Illustrator; Fractal Design Painter; PainterX2

## Techniques:

For this fine art piece, Krause merged a scanned image of a child holding an empty plate with a scan of an old woodcut showing natives retreating in fear as explorers in ships landed on their shores. Using the image of the child as the background, she added a new layer and pasted the woodcut of the natives onto it. She set the Layer Options to Darken mode (to eliminate the white) and the opacity to 50 percent. To super-impose the globe on the plate, but beneath the child's arm, she selected the arm and copied it to another layer. She added a fourth layer and positioned it between the background (of the child) and the layer with the copy of the arm. Pasting the globe onto the fourth layer, she set the mode to Lighten. Creating a final layer posi-tioned above the others Krause pasted the globe again, using Luminosity mode to alter the colors and add a glow to the arm.

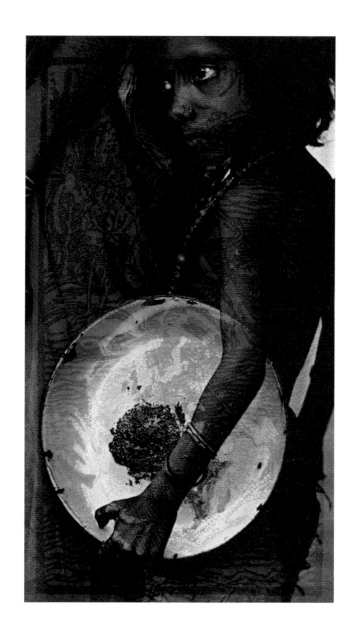

**Artist:** Dorothy Simpson Krause

**Image:** An Empty Plate

**Software:** Photoshop

## Techniques:

Corinne Whitaker has been doing digital fine art on the Macintosh since it first came out, in 1984. Rather than plan her images beforehand, she works intuitively, without any preconceived image in mind. "When I'm all finished I look at it and it tells me what it's about. And that's where the name comes from." This image began as a drawing in Fractal Design Painter, with a black brush on a white background. To add color, Whitaker used Painter's watercolor, pen and charcoal tools. Then she imported the image into Photoshop, where she duplicated it and inverted the duplicate. After copying the duplicate, she pasted it over the original on its own layer. Then she double-clicked on the layer to bring up the Layer Options dialog box, where she set the mode to Dissolve, setting the floating image to 0 and 219 and the underlying image to 62 and 255. Finally, she brought the image back into Painter, where she used the pen to add highlights.

**Artist:** Corinne Whitaker

**Image:** Night Creatures

**Software:** Photoshop; Fractal Design Painter

## Techniques:

This image was a composite of two photos: a closeup of a pearl that Lund shot with a Leaf Digital Camera and a photo of a shell lying on a sheet of iridescent art glass. To darken the top of the image (the shell against the glass), he created a mask that gradated from white at the top to black at the bottom. Next, he reduced Brightness to -50 and increased Saturation to +25. He achieved the rippling effect by applying the ZigZag filter with the Pond ripples option selected, Amount set to 22 and Ridges set to 8.

He selected the pearl, copied and pasted it into the shell image and gave it a Saturation value of +35. The final operation involved creating a shadow just below the pearl. First he dragged down its marquee (Option-Command) and applied a 6-pixel feather to the selection. Then using the pen tool, he created a path around the pearl and subtracted the path (with no feather) from the selection (Paths palette>Make Selection...>Subtract from Selection), which resulted in a soft edge everywhere except where the selection was touching the pearl—there the edge remained hard. Finally, he darkened the selection by moving the Brightness slider all the way to the left.

**Artist:** John Lund, Photodigital

**Image:** Shell on Glass

**Software:** Photoshop

301

Gallery

Torinus created this image for an invitation to a fashion show. To create the watery background texture, she applied the Gaussian Blur filter with a radius of 50 pixels to a 300-dpi scan of satin. After creating an alpha channel of the entire image, she applied Gaussian Blur to that —again set to 50 pixels. To create the appearance of a double image, she offset the channel selection (from the original image) by using the Offset filter with the following settings: Horizontal, 20 pixels right; Vertical, 20 pixels down; Undefined Areas, Wrap Around. Next she used Apply Image in Difference mode to composite the original and the channel selection. This combined with the Offset filter produced a shimmering effect on the background texture.

She then copied a video grab of a ceiling and pasted it into a new layer in Darken mode at 50 percent opacity to create an image that showed areas of both. She next took a video grab of the inside of her computer and pasted that into a new layer using Layer Options—this time with opacity set to 35 percent in Normal mode.

Because the original *FAD Magazine* image (designed by Dean Seven/Richard Stutting; photo by Doris Kloster) was done in FreeHand 3.1, Torinus took a screen capture of it, to preserve the integrity of the type treatment. After reducing its size (which bumped up the resolution) from 72 dpi to 300 dpi, she copied the selection and pasted it into the reflections/ceiling composite. After using the Distort command, she pasted it on a new layer at 50 percent opacity. After applying the Motion blur filter set to 10 pixels, Torinus moved the red channel a few pixels, darkened it and heightened the foreground image's contrast to give it more depth.

**Artist:** Sigi Torinus

**Image:** Fashion Passion

**Software:** Photoshop; FreeHand; Kai's Power Tools

## Techniques:

The artist began by scanning three pen-and-ink sketches of human figures she'd drawn in cross-sections. In Photoshop, she inverted the images using Image>Map>Invert to make the lines white and the backgrounds black. She painted another image in Painter that was to become the background for this composition with Painter's Leaky Pen, Artist Pastel Chalk, the Fat Stroke variant of the airbrush, and the Smeary Mover variant of the Liquid Brush. After rendering some simple geometric objects in Infini-D, she imported them into Photoshop, where she selected each object one by one with the magic wand tool and pasted them onto new layers in the painted background image. She used the Layer Options to set the opacity of the objects. Then she selected areas of the painted background, copied them and pasted them onto a new layer on top of the layer with the geometric shapes. Going back to the original files of the figures, she individually selected and pasted them into another layer positioned above the background and the objects and set the Layer Options to about 65 percent opacity in Multiply mode. For the final touches, she used two KPT filters: KPT Glass Lens Bright to generate the 3D spheres with reflection map, and KPT Julia Set Explorer to create the fractal pasted into the bottom section of the composition.

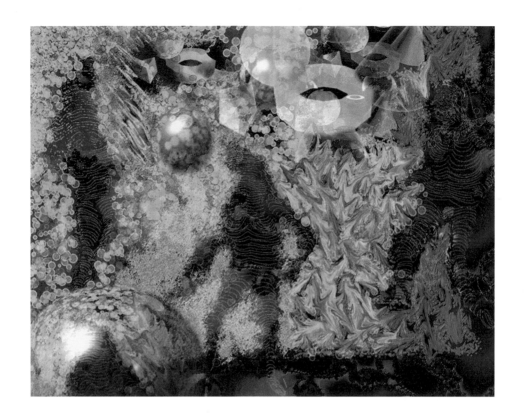

**Artist:** Nance Paternoster

**Image:** Solrlynefigz2

**Software:** Photoshop; Fractal Design Painter; Infini-D; Kai's Power Tools

This image was done for *Psychology Today* magazine to illustrate miraculous recoveries from terminal illnesses. The figure was a photocopy of an x-ray, which Mitsui scanned in Grayscale mode. Because he wanted only red and black for the figure, he switched the mode to Indexed Color. Choosing Color Table under the Mode menu, he highlighted and selected the entire table and chose black for the darkest color and red for the lightest color. This changed all the white areas to red, while leaving all that was black untouched. Then he changed the mode back to RGB.

After saving the hands to an alpha channel, Mitsui loaded the selection and filled it with red at 70 percent opacity, so the purple background beneath it would show through. The background was a piece of satin; just as he'd done with the x-ray, he scanned it as a grayscale image and changed it to Indexed Color, adjusted the color table, then changed the mode to RGB. The radiating lines were drawn in FreeHand, saved in Illustrator 3.0 format and pasted into a Photoshop channel. After loading the channel, Mitsui upped the Brightness setting, and filled it with yellow at 40 percent opacity. The doll and the butterfly were both scanned objects; he used Color Balance to alter their colors by boosting the amount of yellow.

**Artist:** Glenn Mitsui

**Image:** New Miracles

**Software:** Photoshop; FreeHand; Illustrator

## Techniques:

Beginning with a black-and-white photo of a beach scene—which he'd already manipulated in the darkroom, Day switched from grayscale to RGB. Choosing foreground and background colors, he specified a linear blend in Color mode, then adjusted Curves to tweak the colors.

Day opened the second image—a mannequin head—and used Color Range to isolate the head from the background. After making a selection, he feathered it and copied it to the Clipboard. He then pasted the mannequin head into a new channel he'd created in the beach image. Back in RGB mode he loaded the selection of the head and drew another blend, which affected only the selected area. Finally he adjusted the Curves until he achieved the desired colors.

**Artist:** Don Day

**Image:** Ghost at the Beach

**Software:** Photoshop

Day began this image by colorizing a black-and-white photo of a sky by choosing the foreground color and applying a fill in Color mode at 100 percent opacity. The figure—which he used twice at different sizes—also originated as a separate black-and-white image. After using the lasso to separate the figure from the background, he copied it and pasted it into a new layer in the sky file, where he saved the selection to a channel and created a gradient mask. Loading the selection with the gradient, Day created a blend in Color mode going from the foreground to the background color. With the same selection, he created a border of three pixels, feathered the border another five pixels and filled it to create a glowing effect.

Because he wanted to keep a version of the figure to use later, Day copied it to another layer and hid it before merging the first two layers. Using the magic wand and Color Range, he selected highlights of the merged layers so he could put a border around that selection and fill it with a new color. Then he took the second copy of the figure in the layer, added a blend in Color mode and added a border to create a glowing effect. Finally, he scaled it down and flipped it horizontally.

**Artist:** Don Day

**Image:** Hallelujah Sky

**Software:** Photoshop

## Techniques:

Lund first shot a transparency of a sunflower, which he scanned on a drum scanner. After opening the image in Photoshop, he adjusted the brightness and contrast and boosted the saturation by 50 percent. Then he applied the Extrude filter. With the Blocks option selected, he set both Size and Depth values to 35 with the random button checked.

**Artist:** John Lund, Photodigital

**Image:** Sunflower

**Software:** Photoshop

# Section 4

# Resources

# Resources

**addDepth**
Ray Dream Inc.
1804 N. Shoreline Blvd.
Mountain View, CA 94043
(415) 960-0768
(800) 846-0111

A graphics application that adds depth and perspective to line art
and type.
$179 suggested retail.

**Adobe Dimensions**
Adobe Systems, Inc.
1585 Charleston Rd., P.O. Box 7900
Mountain View, CA 94039
(415) 961-4400
(800) 833-6687

PostScript-based graphics program for creating and editing simple
3D objects and effects.
$199 retail.

**Adobe Illustrator**
Adobe Systems, Inc.
1585 Charleston Rd., P.O. Box 7900
Mountain View, CA 94039
(415) 961-4400
(800) 833-6687

Object-oriented PostScript drawing and design program with versa-
tile text handling and high-level color capabilities.
$595 retail.

### Adobe Photoshop
Adobe Systems
1585 Charleston Rd., P.O. Box 7900
Mountain View, CA 94039
(415) 961-4400
(800) 833-6687

Powerful image-creation and photo-manipulation program. New
version includes Layers and sophisticated color controls.
$895 retail.

### Alien Skin
Virtus Corporation
117 Edinburgh St., Ste. 204
Cary, NC 27511
(919) 467-9700

Photoshop plug-in and standalone application that mathematically
generates 2D and 3D textures.
$99 retail.

### Andromeda Filters
Andromeda Software Inc.
699 Hampshire Rd., Ste. 109
Thousand Oaks, CA 91361
(805) 379-4109
(800) 547-0055

Three series of plug-in filters: Series 1 produces special effects by
simulating optical camera lenses; Series 2 lets you wrap two-dimensional images around any of four preset 3D forms, a sphere, a cube,
a cylinder or a 2D plane in 3D space; Series 3 provides a variety of
mezzotint effects.
$129 retail (per series).

### The Black Box
Alien Skin Software
2522 Clark Ave.
Raleigh, NC 27607
(919) 832-4124
America Online: Alien Skin
CompuServe: 72773,777
Internet: alienskin@aol.com

A set of six plug-in filters that add highlights and shadows in and
around selection boundaries.
$89 retail.

**FotoMagic**
Ring of Fire, Inc.
386 Balsam Ave.
Sunnyvale, CA 94086
(415) 967-1828

A set of eight plug-in filters for producing photographic effects.
$195 retail.

**FotoSets**
4104 24th St.
San Francisco, CA 94114
(415) 621-2061
(800) 577-1215

A unique high-end photo library on Photo CD. Contains 100 images
of unusual artistic textures and backgrounds for use in desktop
publishing, illustration and multimedia.
$249 discount price through publisher offer.

**Fractal Design Painter**
Fractal Design Corporation
335 Spreckels Dr.
Aptos, CA 95003
(408) 688-8800
(800) 297-COOL (orders)

24-bit color paint program with sophisticated brush technology and
texture capabilities that simulates natural-media tools.
$399 retail.

**Fractal Design PainterX2**
Fractal Design Corporation
335 Spreckels Dr.
Aptos, CA 95003
(408) 688-8800
(800) 297-COOL (orders)

Expert extension to Fractal Design Painter that allows multiple
floating selections in the same image.
$149 retail.

**Gallery Effects**
Adobe Systems—Seattle
411 First Ave., S.
Seattle, WA 98104
(206) 622-5500
(800) 628-2320

Three separate volumes of plug-in filters (16 filters per volume) that let you apply a variety of photographic and natural-media effects to images.
$149 retail (per volume).

**Image Club Graphics, Inc.**
729 24th Ave., S.E.
Calgary Alberta
CANADA T2G5K8
(800) 661-9410

Catalog of stock photos and images to complement your design library—includes products, fonts, clip art, sample logos, layout ideas and design advice.

**Image Vault**
6506 South Lewis Ave., Ste. 250
Tulsa, OK 74136
(800) 775-4232

Collection of royalty-free high-resolution stock images on photo CD. Compatible with all popular publishing programs and platforms.
$349 retail.

**Kai's Power Tools**
HSC Software
6303 Carpinteria Ave.
Carpinteria, CA 93013
(805) 566-6200
(805) 566-6220 (direct sales)

A set of over 30 special-effects filters—including Texture Explorer and Gradient Designer—for Photoshop and other programs that use plug-in technology.
$199 retail.

**Live Picture**
HSC Software
6303 Carpinteria Ave.
Carpinteria, CA 93013
(805) 566-6200
(805) 566-6220 (direct sales)

Image-editing and compositing program that uses a proprietary
mathematically defined imaging technology to perform data-
intensive manipulations on very large files in near real time.
$3995 retail.

**Paint Alchemy**
Xaos Tools Inc.
600 Townsend St., Ste. 270 E.
San Francisco, CA 94103
(415) 487-7000
(800) 833-9267
internet: macinfo@xaostools.com

Photoshop plug-in with 75 preset styles and 36 controls for creating
customized brush effects.
$99 retail; $109 bundled with Floppy Full of Brushes, a disk of 50
additional brushes ($19.95 sold separately).

**Ray Dream Designer**
Ray Dream Inc.
1804 N. Shoreline Blvd.
Mountain View, CA 94043
(415) 960-0768
(800) 846-0111

3D illustration program that provides 2D-style drawing tools.
$349 suggested retail.

**Specular Collage**
Specular International
479 West St.
Amherst, MA 01002
(413) 253-3100
(800) 433-7732
America Online: specular

Object-oriented image-manipulation tool that allows quick editing
and compositing of low-res proxies in preparation for finalizing the
high-res versions in Photoshop.
$349 retail.

**StrataVision 3D**
Strata Inc.
2 W. Saint George Blvd., Ste. 2100
St. George, UT 84770
(801) 628-5218
(800) 869-6855

A 3D illustration program that includes modeling, scene composition, rendering and animation capabilities.
$995 retail.

**Terrazzo**
Xaos Tools Inc.
600 Townsend St., Ste. 270 E.
San Francisco, CA 94103
(415) 487-7000
(800) 833-9267
internet: macinfo@xaostools.com

Plug-in filter that generates repeating patterns from any PICT or native Photoshop-formatted image in RGB, CMYK or grayscale mode.
$149 retail.

# Contributors

**Erik Adigard:** Educated in France, Adigard attended the University of Censier in Paris, where he studied theories of communication, and later attended the Beaux Arts in Montpellier. Having completed his BFA in graphic design at California College of Arts and Crafts in 1987, he soon opened his own studio, M.A.D., with Patricia McShane in 1989. Erik's work ranges from corporate communications to editorial illustration for clients including national magazines, Silicon Valley start-ups and Fortune 500 companies. His recent projects include illustrations for the Autodesk annual report, introductory spreads for *WIRED*, a campaign for Stop Aids Project, and interface designs for CD-ROM titles. Featured in international publications such as *MDN* (Japan), *Applied Arts* (Canada) and *Industriel Ontwerpen* (Holland), Adigard's designs and illustrations have won numerous awards such as AIGA, CA, Print and STA 100.

**Jim Allman:** A multimedia developer, Allman combines his knowledge of video production, script writing and product design to produce screen graphics and icons for Image Associates in Raleigh, North Carolina. Jim's principal interests lie in education. In the future, he would like to develop interactive media in which onscreen models communicate complex information to people, enhancing the learning experience by exploring the "what if" through illustration and design.

**Stuart Bradford:** Bradford is a San Francisco-based illustrator/ designer who first began using the Macintosh in 1991. A combination of his own photography, found objects and stock images provide the raw material for producing his conceptually driven work. Initially captured by the wonders of Photoshop, he finds himself increasingly interested in line art and natural media effects. His clients include *Macworld*, Stanford University, *Success*, *LAN Times* and *PC World*.

**Annabelle Breakey:** Breakey graduated from the Academy of Art College in San Francisco where she continues to reside and work as a photographer. Working for herself for the past five years, Annabelle began doing digital imaging three years ago. Although her interests are varied, her photography is primarily commercially oriented.

**Jeff Brice:** Brice became interested in technology while a student at Carnegie Mellon. Combining computer technology with his already strong interest in art seemed natural. He has produced photo collages that have appeared in several national exhibitions. Jeff believes that computer technology has allowed him to pursue his interests in photography, painting and fine art simultaneously.

**Don Day:** Day has been a San Francisco Bay area photo-illustrator/graphic artist for 23 years. A 1974 graduate from San Jose State University, he has a BA in Graphic Design with an emphasis in photography and post-graduate courses there in printmaking. After working in print shops, photo labs and graphics production for the screenprinting industry until 1990, he pursued computer graphic design and digital imaging at Foothill College in Los Altas. In 1993, he joined Adobe Systems as technical support specialist and also began teaching computer graphic design at Foothill College. Don has had solo shows of his photography in the Bay area, and continues to work as a digital photographic artist.

**Eve Elberg:** Elberg received her MA in communication design at the Pratt Institute and currently lives in Brooklyn where she focuses on illustration and presentation graphics. Her activities include teaching, consulting and freelance training, and she has recently become an assistant sysop in the Graphics Forum on America Online. Eve is also an active participant in the Photoshop Forum. Her works have been shown in galleries in New York and Montreal. More interested in reaching her viewers on an emotional level than on an intellectual one, Eve uses images to explore and educate, and she strives to create moods and evoke feelings.

**Diane Fenster:** Working in Pacifica, California, Fenster specializes in multilayered, textured illustration and fine art on the Macintosh. With an innovative flair, Diane combines 35mm photography, video and still-video imagery to produce her artwork. Many of her pieces have been exhibited internationally and have appeared in numerous publications on digital imaging. She has also presented her work at various conferences (including the 1994 Photoshop Conference in San Francisco) and has taught at the Center for Creative Imaging in Camden, Maine.

**Helen S. Golden:** After studying in New York, artist-photographer Golden moved to the West Coast, where her work has seen much exposure. In addition to producing her own images, she serves as director of Art Space, a gallery devoted to digital artwork that's part of the Digital Pond, a well-respected San Francisco service bureau. Using a computer has helped Golden, she says, allowing "complex ideas—that were only notions in the past—to be thinkable, then realizable images that I can push further than I ever imagined."

**Wendy Grossman:** A resident of New York City, Grossman runs her own studio, doing illustrations, magazine covers and some advertising work. Some of her art is featured on the CD-ROM that accompanies Adobe Photoshop 3.0. She also teaches courses on Photoshop and Illustrator at New York's School of Visual Arts. Fascinated by the use of unusual output media, Wendy has printed her images on papyrus, fig tree bark, raw silk and other experimental paper alternatives.

**Mitchell Hartman:** After receiving his BFA from the School of Visual Arts in New York City, Hartman became a full-time photo-illustrator. Since starting his own design firm, M Studios, in North White Plains, New York, he has become a nationally known artist.

**Mark Jasin:** A freelance illustrator who runs his own studio—Jasin Design—in Denver, Jasin earned his BFA in graphic design from Arizona State University and worked as an editorial illustrator in California before settling in Colorado. His artwork has appeared in several computer-related books. Mark sees Photoshop as a powerful tool that opens up a wide range of opportunities within the commercial graphic arts field. "Photoshop," he declares, "is the most sophisticated program out there."

**Ruth Kedar:** After receiving a BS in architecture and town planning from the Israeli Institute of Technology, Kedar went on to earn an MFA from Stanford University. Currently teaching design at Stanford, Kedar recently co-founded Art on the Net, an art exhibition accessible through the World Wide Web on the Internet. An award-winning designer, she has designed a number of playing card decks, including her best-known, Analog. Many of her digitally designed cards were showcased in the typography magazine, *U & lc*. Ruth works on many layers—literally and figuratively—developing, as she explains, "logical structures that create new visual progressions. The creative process, this dialogue between self and medium, evolves into visual languages—their grammar ever changing to encompass new avenues of thought. Therefore, my medium of choice is always a vehicle of variation and exploration."

**Dorothy Simpson Krause:** Krause is currently the artist-in-residence at the Center for Creative Imaging, on sabbatical from teaching computer graphics in the Department of Design at the Massachusetts College of Art. Krause received her doctorate from Pennsylvania State University.  Her work has been displayed in a number of solo and group exhibitions and has been published in several industry magazines. Dr. Krause feels that "electronic media enables us to transcend our separateness and to understand, as at no point in the past, our interdependence."

**Kai Krause:** Executive vice president of HSC Software, Kai is the "Kai" of Kai's Power Tools, HSC's award-winning set of extensions and filters for Adobe Photoshop and other compatible plug-in programs. Recognized as one of the world's leading imaging experts, Krause is well known for his incredible "human interface" designs. Besides Kai's Power Tools, Krause lent his expertise to interfaces for HSC's new KPT Bryce, a 3D landscape terrain generation program, and Live Picture, the revolutionary imaging software published in North America by HSC.

**Mark Landman:** An independently self-taught artist residing in Cotati, California, Landman's illustrations have appeared in magazines such as *Mondo 2000, Time, M* and *Heavy Metal* and have been commissioned by such publishers as Apple Computer Discovery Group, Mystic Fire Video and Kitchen Sink Press. Mark was a speaker at the 1994 San Francisco Photoshop Conference, where he discussed third-party filters. The piece featured in *Photoshop f/x* was first seen in *Mondo* and has since been altered and mutated with Photoshop tricks, which allow for the creative expression of the artist's free will.

**Bonny Lhotka:** Lhotka received her BFS from Bradley University and now works as a full-time artist in original acrylic painting and digital media. Adding her twenty-five years of experience in painting and print-making techniques to computer technology, Lhotka creates unique pieces that are displayed in over one hundred major corporations, including United Airlines, AT&T, Johnsons Space Center and the U.S. State Department. Working on commission for national designers, Bonny has also worked internationally in Japan, South Africa and New Guinea. She approaches her art intuitively and spontaneously, seldom keeping records of how any one piece is created, "preferring instead to take advantage of accidents, allowing each piece to grow step by step."

**John Lund:** An advertising photographer of twenty years, Lund began working with photodigital media four years ago. A regular contributor to Macworld Expositions, John has also had his work profiled in *Computer Artist, Photo District News* and *Popular Photography,* among other magazines. Founder of Photodigital Imaging in San Francisco, John praises the merits of computer technology. "Computers are the most incredibly creative tool ever given to a photographer, allowing one to eliminate the barriers between imagination and execution."

**Kent Manske:** An associate professor of Art & Visual Communication at Foothill College, Manske lives and works in the lower San Francisco Bay area. His credentials include an MFA from the School of the Art Institute of Chicago. Kent's works have been shown in both solo and group exhibitions, and are a part of several permanent collections, including that of Texas A&M University. Manske's inspiration arises from emotional and intellectual introspections about the human condition and everyday existence.

**Patricia McShane:** McShane, a native of San Francisco, studied fine art and photography at San Francisco State University and graphic design at California College of Arts & Crafts. In 1989 she and French designer, Erik Adigard, formed M.A.D., a studio involved in graphic design, illustrating and multimedia projects. Currently, Patricia is designing calendars, book covers, outdoor graphics and interface designs for CD-ROM titles. Her work has achieved international exposure, appearing in publications such as *MDN* and *Super Design* (Japan), *Novum* (Germany) and *Studio Magazine* (Canada). Some of McShane's clients include Autodesk, Adobe Systems, Apple Computer, Harper Collins Publishing and Turner Network Television.

**Judy L. Miller:** After getting a Master's in Fine Arts from the University of Iowa in 1976, Miller embarked on an art and design career that included a strong emphasis on printing. Her work is part of a number of permanent collections, largely in Texas, including the Dallas Museum of Art. The winner of several design awards, Judy has been a freelance artist/illustrator since 1986.

**Glenn Mitsui:** Mitsui is a visiting faculty member for the Pacific Center of Imaging and an Instructor for United Digital Artists. He has received a number of awards, including Graphis and the Seattle Design Association. Glenn got his start with Boeing Computer Services, where he worked in both the design and computer graphics groups. In 1989 he co-founded Studio M D, which currently generates artwork for such clients as Microsoft, Apple and Aldus.

**Bert Monroy:** Born and raised in New York City, Monroy spent twenty years in the advertising industry as an art director before embarking on a new digital career with the introduction of the Macintosh in 1984. Embracing the computer as an artistic medium, Monroy has produced pieces that have been featured in numerous publications such as *Macworld, MacUser, The Photoshop WOW Book* and *The Gray Book*. He also coauthored the award-winning *Official Adobe Photoshop Handbook.* An accomplished teacher and lecturer, Bert has served on the faculty of The School of Visual Arts, Center for Creative Imaging, College of Arts & Crafts. He currently teaches at San Francisco State University. Having recently relocated to the San Francisco Bay area, he and his partner, David Biedny, have set up a full service multimedia production studio handling interactive as well as linear presentations.

**Corinne Okada:** Okada is a San Francisco artist working in both digital and traditional media. She has guest lectured at Foothill College and at Stanford University. Her works have appeared in *PRINT Magazine, Computer Pictures Magazine, OnLine Design* and *MacUser.* Her clients include Apple Computer, Silicon Graphics and NeXT Computer. Corinne's work is influenced by her diverse background; her mother is of German and Welsh descent from the South, and her father is third-generation Japanese from Hawaii.

**Nance Paternoster:** Paternoster has a BFA from Syracuse, and an MA from San Francisco State, both in digital artistry. She currently teaches at the Academy of Art College, in San Francisco. Throughout her career, she has been combining computer graphics with other media, mainly due to limitations in technology. From a humble beginning with hand-colored photocopies Nance has escalated her activities to the point where her focus has become the manipulation of computer-generated images viewed through light sculptures of neon and glass.

**David Peters:** Peters received a BFA from Cal State Sonoma in 1972, and continued his education by traveling through Europe, the Middle East and Asia. His work has been presented at exhibitions around the world, including the Torpedo Factory Gallery, in Alexandria, Virginia, and La Foret Museum, in Tokyo, Japan. David also does commercial work for clients such as ABC-TV, Disney and *Newsweek*. Peters is also an avid collector of mid-twentieth-century kitsch, contemporary art and artifacts.

**Steven Soshea:** Since earning his BFA in design from California College of Arts & Crafts, Soshea has produced illustrations for such publications such as *PRINT Magazine Regional, Design Annual* and *Stars and Stripes.* In addition, Steven's work is on display in both small businesses and national corporations throughout the United States. Steven describes his work as an exploration of the inner passions, desires, wills and workings of the mind combined with historical allegories, icons and a contemporary vernacular.

**David Teich:** A full-time illustrator in Roosevelt, New Jersey, Teich has been successfully running his own business, Mind of the Machine, for the past two years. His illustrations have been profiled in journals including *Popular Science, Consumer Reports, Step-by-Step Electronic Design* and *Money* and his clients include HBO, AT&T and Absolut Vodka. His work is influenced not only by his lifelong interest in making art, but also by his experience in printing and typography before computers came into the picture. Commenting on his work, David says, "I try to focus on the idea and not get lost in the glitz of the technology, although I'm totally committed to working on the computer. Most of all, I try to have fun with it."

**Sigi Torinus:** Born in the Virgin Islands, Torinus studied in Germany before being awarded a Fulbright Scholarship for Fine Arts, in San Francisco. Torinus's works have been shown around the world, in exhibitions/performances in Germany, Russia, Mexico and in several cities in the United States.

**Richard Tuschman:** Previously a graphic designer, Tuschman is now a full-time illustrator in Pearl River, New York. Widely published, Richard's work has appeared in *Newsweek, Sports Illustrated, The New Yorker* and *Macworld.* With an equally impressive client list, he has done work for Adobe, Microsoft, Doubleday and Random House. Having come to illustration late in life, Tuschman hopes in his work to bring some sense of fine art to the commercial marketplace.

**Greg Vander Houwen:** Vander Houwen is the owner of Interact, a small computer graphics firm located just outside of Seattle. Experienced in video, computers, photography and apple farming, Greg trains and lectures on electronic imaging, retouching and digital illustration. He is also a regular speaker at Photoshop conferences. His fine art has been shown internationally and will be featured on the Photoshop 3.0 CD. His work makes him popular with his clients, which include Apple Computer, Adobe Systems and Microsoft.

**Corinne Whitaker:** A Carmel artist working in digital imaging, Whitaker's has had her artwork featured in reviews and publications such as *The Power of Art, Computer Graphics World, Los Angeles Times* and *New York Times.* Her award-winning work can be seen in permanent collections in NASA, the Museum of Photographic Arts in San Diego and the Society for Contemporary Photography in Kansas City, Missouri. A dedicated artist who has shown her art in galleries across the nation, Corinne feels that digital imaging is revolutionary. "No one can yet foresee the outcome: maybe silicon bodies and carbon bodies will merge; maybe Johnny can't spell because our linear alphabet is archaic; maybe geography will be redefined as immersion in a mindspace. Digital art leads us to that awesome and profound frontier where tomorrow parts company with today."

**Nanette Wylde:** Wylde was recently honored by the California Arts Council, as the CSMA Artist-in-Residence for 1994. In addition to producing art work, Nanette works as an Arts in Action teacher at the Community School of Music and Art and as a tapestry artist/facilitator at Tapestry and Talent of San Jose. Her works have been displayed in both solo exhibitions and group shows throughout the golden state.

**Mark Yankus:** Yankus is a successful New York-based illustrator. He first became interested in computer-assisted art after fiddling with a Mac Plus in Macy's. He saw the tremendous potential of the medium, especially in his area of specialization, collage. Despite all his work in digital media, Mark doesn't consider himself a computer artist; rather, he views the computer as a tool. With this tool, he hopes one day to bring his dreams of animated art to fruition, with the eventual ability to enter the works and explore a new space where virtual reality meets fine art.

# Index

**333**

335

# Colophon

The *Photoshop f/x* book was produced on a variety of Macintosh machines, including a IIsi, IIci, Quadra 650 and Quadra 700. Page proofs were printed on a Hewlett Packard LaserJet 4M Plus and an Apple LaserWriter Pro.

QuarkXPress 3.3 was used for all layout. Images were produced by individual artists primarily using Photoshop 3.0. Graphics were produced using Photoshop 3.0.

Body copy is Palatino, heads are Univers and BureauEmpire.

# MACINTOSH

## Explore Cyberspace!

*The Mac Internet Tour Guide*
$27.95
350 pages, illustrated
ISBN: 1-56604-062-0

Mac users can now navigate the Internet the easy way: by pointing and clicking, dragging and dropping. In easy-to-read, entertaining prose, Internet expert Michael Fraase leads you through installing and using the software enclosed in the book to send and receive e-mail, transfer files, search the Internet's vast resources and more! BONUS: Free trial access and two free electronic updates.

## Handy 3-in-1 Guide!

*Mac, Word & Excel Desktop Companion, Second Edition*
$24.95
308 pages, illustrated
ISBN: 1-56604-130-9

Why clutter your desk with three guides? This money saver gets you up and running with Apple's System 7.1 software and the latest versions of Microsoft Word and Excel for the Mac. A complete overview, examples of each program's commands, tools and features and step-by-step tutorials guide you easily along the learning curve for maximum Macintosh productivity!

## Software $avings!

*The Mac Shareware 500, Second Edition*
$34.95
504 pages, illustrated
ISBN: 1-56604-076-0

This book is a fantastic reference for any designer or desktop publisher interested in saving money by using the vast resources shareware offers. Literally thousands of fonts, graphics, clip-art files and utilities are available for downloading via dozens of online services. To get you started, this book includes two disks of shareware.

# Macintosh

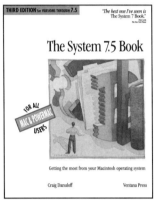

## Now for System 7.5!

*The System 7.5 Book, Third Edition*
$24.95
728 pages, illustrated
ISBN: 1-56604-129-5

The all-time bestselling *System 7 Book*, now revised, updated and re-titled! With over 120,000 copies in print, *The System 7.5 Book* is the industry's recognized standard and the last word on the Macintosh and PowerMac operating systems. A complete overview of AppleHelp, AOCE, e-mail, fax, PC Exchange, MacTCP, QuickTime and more!

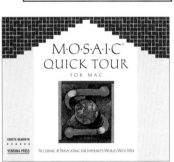

## Cruise the World Wide Web!

*Mosaic Quick Tour for Mac*
$12.00
208 pages, illustrated
ISBN: 1-56604-195-3

The *Mosaic Quick Tour* introduces the how-to's of hypertext travel in a simple, picturesque guide, allowing you to view linked text, audio and video resources thousands of miles apart. You can use Mosaic to do all of your information hunting and gathering, including Gopher searches, newsgroup reading and file transfers through FTP.

## Become a Voodoo Guru!

*Voodoo Mac, Second Edition*
$24.95
400 pages, illustrated
ISBN: 1-56604-177-5

Whether you're a power user looking for new shortcuts or a beginner trying to make sense of it all, *Voodoo Mac* has something for everyone! Computer veteran Kay Nelson has compiled hundreds of invaluable tips, tricks, hints and shortcuts that simplify your Macintosh tasks and save time, including disk and drive magic, font and printing tips, alias alchemy and more!

# Welcome to the *Photoshop f/x Online Companion!*

Wouldn't it be great if a book as informative as *Photoshop f/x* never had to end? Well, it doesn't have to. With the *Photoshop f/x Online Companion* you have a never-ending source of valuable information.

The *Photoshop f/x Online Companion* is an informative tool, as well as an annotated software library. It offers full text searching of the premiere Photoshop mailing list where both professional and amateurs gather in an electronic forum to discuss the latest secrets and cool new tricks of the trade, as well as to answer fundamental questions in an easy-to-understand way. So with this *Online Companion* you're never out of the loop!

The *Photoshop f/x Online Companion* also links you to Internet clip art, an offering that enables you to browse through the various Internet sites where cutting-edge art and electronic know-how meet.

Perhaps one of the most impressive features of the *Online Companion* is the Software Archive. Here, you'll find and be able to download the latest versions of all the software mentioned in *Photoshop f/x* that are freely available on the Net. This software ranges from Photo CD, a new method for storing photographs digitally on CD-ROM, to graphics filters created by Chris Cox that allow you to solarize, equalize and experiment with fractal noise. Also, with its handy before-and-after visual guide, you'll be able to judge which software is most suited to your project so you won't download the software just to find you have no use for it.

The *Photoshop f/x Online Companion* also links you to the Ventana Library where you will find useful press and jacket information as well as other Ventana Press offerings. Plus, you have access to a wide selection of exciting new releases and coming attractions. In addition, Ventana's Online Library allows you to order the books you want.

The *Photoshop f/x Online Companion* represents Ventana Online's ongoing commitment to offering the most dynamic and exciting products possible. And soon Ventana Online will be adding more services, including more multimedia supplements, searchable indices and sections of the book reproduced and hyperlinked to the Internet resources they reference.

To access, connect via the World Wide Web to
**http://www.vmedia.com/photoshopfx.html**

# DESIGN AND CONQUER!

## Looking Good With QuarkXPress

$34.95
350 pages, illustrated
ISBN: 1-56604-148-1
Harness QuarkXPress's superior publishing power with an emphasis on good design and using the right tools. Looking Good With QuarkXPress makes "looking good" a practical matter, combining design ideas with tips on using XPress's tools to achieve special effects. Tough topics are cleared up, shortcuts and commands are grouped in easy-to-use tables and practical examples abound. Available in November.

## Advertising From the Desktop

$24.95
427 pages, illustrated
ISBN: 1-56604-064-7
*Advertising From the Desktop* offers unmatched design advice and helpful how-to instructions for creating persuasive ads. With tips on how to choose fonts, select illustrations, apply special effects and more, this book is an idea-packed resource for improving the looks and effects of your ads.

## The Presentation Design Book, Second Edition

$24.95
320 pages, illustrated
ISBN: 1-56604-014-0
*The Presentation Design Book* is filled with thoughtful advice and instructive examples for creating business presentation visuals, including charts, overheads, type, etc., that help you communicate and persuade. The *Second Edition* adds advice on the use of multimedia. For use with any software or hardware.

## The Gray Book, Second Edition

$24.95
262 pages, illustrated
ISBN: 1-56604-073-6
This "idea gallery" for desktop publishers offers a lavish variety of the most interesting black, white and gray graphic effects that can be achieved with laser printers, scanners and high-resolution output devices. The *Second Edition* features new illustrations, synopses and steps, added tips and an updated appendix.

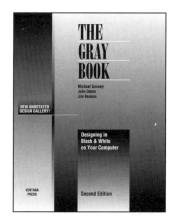

## Looking Good in Print, Third Edition

$24.95
412 pages, illustrated
ISBN: 1-56604-047-7
For use with any software or hardware, this desktop design bible has become the standard among novice and experienced desktop publishers alike. With over 300,000 copies in print, *Looking Good in Print* is even better, with new sections on photography and scanning. Learn the fundamentals of professional-quality design along with tips on resources and reference materials.

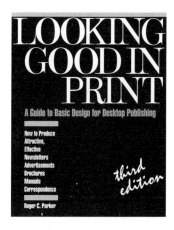

## Newsletters From the Desktop, Second Edition

$24.95
306 pages, illustrated
ISBN: 1-56604-133-3
Now the millions of desktop publishers who produce newsletters can learn how to improve the design of their publications. Filled with helpful design tips and illustrations, as well as hands-on tips for building a great looking publication. Includes an all-new color gallery of professionally designed newsletters, offering publishers at all levels a wealth of ideas and inspiration.

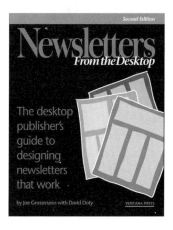

---

## Can't wait to order?  We understand. Call toll-free:

# 800/743-5369 (U.S. only)

# To order any Ventana Press title, fill out this order form and mail it to us with payment for quick shipment.

| | Quantity | | Price | | Total |
|---|---|---|---|---|---|
| *The Mac Internet Tour Guide* | _____ | x | $27.95 | = | $ _____ |
| *Mac, Word & Excel Desktop Companion, 2nd Edition* | _____ | x | $24.95 | = | $ _____ |
| *The Mac Shareware 500, 2nd Edition* | _____ | x | $34.95 | = | $ _____ |
| *The System 7.5 Book, 3rd Edition* | _____ | x | $24.95 | = | $ _____ |
| *Mosaic Quick Tour for Mac* | _____ | x | $12.00 | = | $ _____ |
| *Voodoo Mac, 2nd Edition* | _____ | x | $24.95 | = | $ _____ |
| *Looking Good With QuarkXPress* | _____ | x | $34.95 | = | $ _____ |
| *Advertising From the Desktop* | _____ | x | $24.95 | = | $ _____ |
| *The Presentation Design Book, 2nd Edition* | _____ | x | $24.95 | = | $ _____ |
| *The Gray Book, 2nd Edition* | _____ | x | $24.95 | = | $ _____ |
| *Looking Good in Print, 3rd Edition* | _____ | x | $24.95 | = | $ _____ |
| *Newsletters From the Desktop, 2nd Edition* | _____ | x | $24.95 | = | $ _____ |

|  |  |  |
|---|---|---|
| | Subtotal = | $ _____ |

SHIPPING:
For all regular orders, please <u>add</u> $4.50/first book, $1.35/each additional. = $ _____
For "two-day air," <u>add</u> $8.25/first book, $2.25/each additional. = $ _____
For orders to Canada, <u>add</u> $6.50/book. = $ _____
For orders sent C.O.D., <u>add</u> $4.50 to your shipping rate. = $ _____
North Carolina residents must <u>add</u> 6% sales tax. = $ _____
International orders must pay additional charges.  TOTAL = $ _____

Name_____  Company_____

Address (No PO Box)_____

City_____ State_____ Zip _____

Daytime Telephone _____

___ Payment enclosed ___VISA ___MC  # _____Exp. Date _____

Signature _____

Mail or fax to: Ventana Press, PO Box 2468, Chapel Hill, NC 27515  ☎ 919/942-0220  Fax 919/942-1140

## CAN'T WAIT? CALL OR FAX TOLL-FREE
## ☎ 800/743-5369  FAX 800/877-7955  (U.S. only)

PFX001